# Lost Angels

*Also by the Author*

College Survival Guide: You Are Not Alone

# Lost Angels

*Encounters with First Nations*

Paula Laureen Henderson

Gundrop Enterprise

Edited by

Mary E. H. Hilger
Rosemarie Stalker
Shirley Collingridge-Word Smith

For more information:
www.gumdropenterprises.com

Printed and Bound in Canada

ISBN 978-0-9783141-1-8

# Dedication

This book is dedicated to my grandpa, Paul Mudryk, a man who phones me every year on my birthday. He is there when everyone else has given up on me. Thank you is not enough.

This book is also in memory of my Auntie, Karen Mudryk. Karen reminded me, the month before she died, when an artist does not create she is dead already. Karen lived.

# Acknowledgments

Jesus, Thank-you for teaching me to dream, this world has nothing for me.

Father- Thank you for being fearless

Mother- Thank you for humming because you are happy

Glen Scrimshaw-When I was young, I would sit on the couch and stare at your print hanging on our wall. It has always been a dream of mine to have one of your *visions of the north* on the cover of my book. Thank you for making a life long dream come true!

Mary E. H. Hilger- Your excellence and selflessness has always inspired me. You keep working when everyone else has quit. Thank you Mary for walking with me on every journey. I know that you are going to be a profound mother!

Doris Overbo- Thank you for giving me a place to call home. Only God in heaven will be able to thank you for all the sacrifices you have made for me. I will try, but it won't compare to your giving heart.

Nita Carvalho-Thank you for reminding me to always go back to the beginning. You are right, the answer is always waiting there for me.

Shelley Liu-You are my sanity. I am sorry Shelley with an *e*, a second book is nothing like a second pregnancy.

Bill and Glory Craig-Thank you for answering the phone, making me yummy honey chicken, your wise advice, and most of all-for teaching me to be frugalicious babe.

Jeffrey G. Benson- Thank you for asking me *what I was going to do with all those stories*. You made me mad.

Yvonne Henderson- Thank you Yvonne for being supportive when I needed you most! I am so proud of all you have accomplished this year.

# Table of Contents

# Chapter one

# Qualified

# Waiting

The golden plains, where warriors once stood, now sparkled with a blanket of snow, welcoming winter. As I drove my still cold vehicle through the city of Saskatoon for my interview, my teeth chattered. While weaving in and out of hostile traffic, I noticed the increase in wait times at each traffic light. Thankful that I was leaving THIS community under construction, I sipped my coffee with a sense of victory. The rent increases coming in the new year were monstrous, attacking my hope for success as an artist. Doubling in cost, housing market prices were breaking the resolve of middle class residents. Once called the culture capital of Canada, our growing city was now also being hailed as a corporate success story.

Desperate to find a parking stall near the front doors of the college, I frantically circled the block. There was nothing enjoyable about minus thirty degrees Celsius weather. Fearful that I was late for my appointment, I hustled from my SUV into the building like a frightened student.

Out of breath, as I reached the desk, I whispered, "May I please speak with Vince, oh, I cannot remember his last name."

With professional annoyance, the attractive secretary stated Vince's last name, asking me to take a seat.

Breaking the bleak monotony of the clean, gray, institutional office were the beautiful pieces of artwork created by First Nations people. The perfectly framed paintings were alluring, often appearing abstract to those ignorant of the Native culture. A cabin, perfectly rendered, peaceful in snow-covered fields, made me wonder where the artist was hiding. Perhaps he lived on his reserve; perhaps he had a city loft, defying stereotypes.

Straining to inspect spruce-like trees, I was distracted by a young man. He seemed as agitated about waiting as I was. Scruffy, with long unkempt hair pulled back in a ponytail, a red hoodie, and jeans about to slide off his thick waist, his blank stare said little fazed him. Tapping his pen, this fellow student wondered when he would be called.

"Do you know who won?" I asked.

He gazed at me, perplexed, not sure whether to answer or to look down.

He waited for a less confrontational approach. Forgetting that First Nations students do not ask questions with emotion, I rephrased my question.

"The football game that was on television last night – who won the finals?" I asked, avoiding eye contact. "I don't have a television."

"You could have just gone to a sports bar and watched the game," he advised me for future reference. How could anyone not know who won the most important football game in the last 20 years?

"Did you not see everyone partying like crazy?" he chided. "We won!" he declared boldly. "Saskatchewan won the Grey Cup!"

"Did I miss a good game?" I said with hope, as

though I might have been part of the community victory.

"Oh," he looked down. "It was a tight game, close, really close." Trying to hide his pride and his smile, he turned away.

Noticing the tattoos and markings on his exposed arm, I wondered which program he was studying. Many students walked the halls at the Saskatchewan Indian Institute of Technology, and most looked excited. Some of the young men had long hair like his; others had short hair; they all dressed like corporate hopefuls. The women had long beautiful black hair, and smoldering feminine eyes. Most muttered as they stepped into the Arctic-like outdoors. I perceived they were probably freshmen, still looking for their own voice.

Freshmen tend to wander through the cafeteria, dazed by their first exam week. They look unsure and few are willing to interact with others at their table or to debate what they have learned. Absorbing so much information their first year, they focus on simply staying alert.

The office administrators where I patiently waited tuned out the students. They busily answered phones and filed folders. Others had their doors shut to protect the privacy of the students they counseled. The office bustled like any educational institution, serious professionals on a mission. As a team, the administrators and teachers would train students who wanted a ticket, qualifying them for employment. They had a mandate, a vision, and most had degrees, as evidenced by framed diplomas proudly displayed along with family photos.

"Paula?" I was softly called to my appointment. I followed Mr. Morrisette toward his office down the hall, past people who occasionally looked up to welcome the stranger with eye contact. In his office, I noticed photos of students and a plaque they had given him. Carved in wood, the words "Thank you for believing in us," spoke of his ability. I looked about the well-organized room, noting the desk situated to look out the window and face guests at the same time. On his desk displaying names scratched in boxes, his calendar revealed that the trades instructor was a people person and a visionary.

## The Builder

I did not want to expose my inadequacy as an unorganized writer, so I quickly dug for the pen and paper stashed in my pocket, rummaging like an absent-minded professor lost in thought. I wasn't sure if Vince minded my coffee thermos on his desk, but the shiny mug immediately relaxed formalities.

The winter wind had blown my hair in front of my eyes, and the cold air had dried my damp curls. I knew I was ill-prepared for this interview and began to ask questions even before recovering my tools.

Vince spoke with an ease – a boldness even – that most professionals will use with interviewers. He was calm, his voice ringing with authority made more noticeable by the Cree accent. He handed me a pen as I scooted my chair closer to the desk. He also offered me paper, encouraging me to take notes. Family photos on the wall seemed to have more precedence than his accolades, which distracted me. He was intrigued by my writing style after speaking with me on the phone, and seemed genuinely interested in why I asked the questions that I did. Informing him that I recently learned that screwdrivers have different heads; his lessons on *house building* required repetition.

He seemed completely mesmerized by my distraction, my need for random answers with little sequence. I simply wanted to understand his role, what his position entailed, and how it affected the growing economy. I wanted to discern if the upcoming election issues were of any interest to his age group, and how he would interpret them from his cultural background. Instead, I encountered a professional tradesman, explaining the difference between a house and a home.

Clad in dress pants and dress shirt, his hair was short, and a masculine ring flashed on his finger as he moved his hand. He was a sharp contrast to the student I had met in the waiting room. A teacher and administrator, he was concerned about where the students had come from and where they were going. Training, guiding, and qualifying a student was a process, he said, a cycle you have to be willing and bold enough to engage in. Explaining his mandate and function, he reminded me that students must come prepared and be academically able to handle the material and the expectations of the workforce.

Without allowing me to preface my interview or explain my article, he began to assure me that the school had an achievable mandate. He had allotted me an hour. He would need every minute as he described the students – where they came from, what they have overcome, how they will succeed. As a writer who graduated with an administration degree, I was startled by his direction, yet intrigued. Visionaries often feel the need to preface and direct a conversation in order to maximize time, making an appointment efficient. He quickly assured me, while I began asking questions, that he was not going to set up young students for failure. He was going to insist they were qualified with the education they needed. I stared at him blankly, not comprehending his meaning of "qualified."

Vince leaned back in his chair, grimacing. I wondered whether his facial expression was in response to my ignorance or his need to be thorough on a limited time budget.

"Seriously, sir," I said with sincerity, "what do you mean by qualified?" remembering the hole I had made in my wall, mistakenly believing I was efficient with a hammer.

As Vince collected his thoughts, I rummaged through my pockets for a candy cane to munch. I often had leftover Christmas candies in my pockets for what I viewed emergencies: long meetings, cold winter days, bad breath, and awkward moments. Vince gazed at me as though I were an awkward detective trying to interrogate him.

Smiling with assurance, he handed me more paper. Impressed by his instinct that I would need more paper, I sat straighter hoping to convey that my tool inadequacies did not reflect my ability to write.

"Qualified, Paula," he said slowly and methodically, "is when you build a house and it is done right."

## How to Build a Home

Vince explained how well-made houses are well designed, and windows and walls prevent moisture from building up. When rushed or careless builders let moisture into a house through their poor craftsmanship, they created an environment for black mould. Once black mould infests a house, it will soon spread to the furniture, clothes, bedding, and cherished belongings.

I was not offended by his simplified explanation because I really did not understand construction, house building, or who should or should not earn a builder's ticket. I recalled black mould problem on some reserves. When many people live in one house, the plumbing is used more frequently, increasing humidity. In a poorly built house, this environment creates black mould. I remembered hearing about a couple of houses being burned down once the problem became unsolvable.

"What do people do?" I interrupted, impatient at his thorough explanation. "What do they do if the house is infested? What do they do when the roof caves in?"

He looked vexed, his eyes piercing mine. "They take their toothbrush and leave," he replied simply.

My heart sank. That was it, they leave. As I briefly lived on the reserves over the holidays, I remembered how their situation reminded me of hurricane victims seen on television. These victims were left homeless, cold, clinging to a toothbrush, as they left their homes and wandered over the reservation to find a place to rest. I did not understand why the loss of a house did not rate media attention. I was confused as to why they were not considered victims of tragedy in Canada, when clearly they were to the United Nations.

I was also confused as to why people were just asked to leave. Did the reserves not have funding to build mould-free houses? Then I remembered studying statistics as a Public Administration student. The average household lives on less than $10 thousand a year. If they lose their house, they would not have finances in the middle of winter for emergencies. I slumped in my seat, knowing that few who read our national press would ever see the results of this poor decision-making.

To encourage me, Vince began to explain that it is important to take pride in my craft. That is why he wants his students to achieve excellence – because their decisions will affect families and communities. When builders take shortcuts, people go homeless. Being qualified for a task is important; work done well is imperative. His passion made his eyes shine.

On an envelope and computer paper, he drew four lines. Ensuring I was paying attention, he showed me how builders run strings and drop lines to secure footings.

"Is that so the tractors did not tip over?" I asked.

He could see he needed to start from the beginning. He began again. If a person on the reserve wants to build a house, they cannot just build wherever they please. First, they make a request at the band office, where they are put on a waiting list. Until 50 years ago, most First Nations people built cabins, with only a wood stove keeping them warm in sub-Arctic weather. Their cabins were made with ill-fitting logs cut down in the forest and held together with mud and straw. He chuckled as he told me how his father bought their first home by trading his wedding suit for a cabin. As children came along, he simply lifted the roof and added rooms.

Politics and technology have changed and First Nations people on reservations now ask the band for a house, which is subsidized by the government. Once their site is approved, excavation begins. Ground soil is cleared down to virgin earth. With a father's gaze, Vince explained a house cannot be built on dirt that has been shuffled around. Only virgin ground was strong enough to hold the weight of a new home.

To prepare the footing, builders use a transit. *Hmm, a transit – a city bus?* I wondered silently. The more he described tools, the more his eyes seemed to twinkle, like a child at Christmas unwrapping a package. A transit, is a tool that helps builders make ninety-degree angles, he explained – or they can use a plumb bob to establish corners below grade. *Please, Lord, do not let him confuse me by going on a tangent,* I silently prayed.

As I picked cat hair off my fleece jacket, he realized he was losing me. He drew a footing to help me visualize, explaining it has to be twice the width of the foundation. "Hopefully that happens on the reserve," he added.

Footings are officially inspected to ensure they meet the regulations. The only reason a reservation house would have problems with its footing would be if the inspector was privately hired and passed an improperly poured footing. "Footings should be approved by the CMHC," he insisted. "They are very good at upholding the standard."

Next comes the foundation. He captured my attention by bending an envelope to represent the foundation. While concrete foundations are best, rural communities are often far from concrete outlets; most foundations in the North are constructed of wood.

*Wood would rot, would it not?* I wondered. Anticipating my question, he began drawing around the foundation.

The wood must be treated and the wall should be constructed of 2x6's. Nails must be galvanized and it is imperative that the foundation be sealed with a waterproof membrane. Of course residents would have preferred the sturdier concrete foundations, but why argue when the house is free?

Next, weeping tile surrounds the foundation. Eighty percent of reservation houses do not have sewers. Instead, they have a sump or "septic tank". If crushed rock is not around the tank liner, dirt seeps into the tank and gets caught in the sump pump. With few repairmen on isolated reserves, a damage can mean no relief for the household.

Above the crushed rock lies the buffer zone, needed because when the weather changes, the ground contracts and expands. With no buffer zone, these temperature changes would bend the walls. Like relationships, with no buffer zone, the foundation deteriorates.

When pouring cement, there has to be a water stop right in the middle, a piece of rubber eight inches wide. Rebar is expensive, which is why some contractors scrimp on it. If the basement is cement and shortcuts have been taken to save costs, the living quarters could become flooded.

"Concrete has to be vibrated," he explained. "If not, little pockets occur where the water seeps in."

"Would a journeyman cut corners on a house, and risk the value of the home like that?" I asked sarcastically.

The room fell instantly quiet as he stared at me with intensity, prompting memories of my father's reprimands, so I sat straight in my chair hoping to appease him. My mouth went dry and I braced myself for a similar angry lecture.

"Do not be naïve, Paula!" scolded Vince. "Many men have sacrificed their houses for money. In the pursuit of flipping a house and a quick buck, they destroy the value of their home."

"Why would they sacrifice their own residence?" I asked submissively.

"They are not building a home, they are building a house. They are making a dwelling place that never had a foundation to be permanent. Men with integrity build a home, unlike boys wanting profit at any cost," he said.

It was apparent that he had learned a sound work ethic while growing up. Perhaps sensing that I thought he was harsh, he began to relate his own life history.

Vince's parents had attended residential schools and were determined their children undergo the same working experience. His mother was strict, and would not let him sit idle as a teenager. He would have to work and pay his own bills by the labor of his hands. His mother was not lazy and she would not tolerate a lazy son.

Instead of being sent to an institutional school, Vince attended public school in a northern Saskatchewan town. "Were you treated well there?" I asked.

As he looked down, I could see sorrow replacing the calm, assured gaze I had seen at the beginning of our conversation. He said, quietly, that the kids were just as mean at public school – calling out racial slurs and condemning him. He was unwelcome and uninspired by a school not yet prepared for racial differences.

As he continued to tell his history, his voice shook. He had seemed so strong, yet he had scars like his peers, scars evidenced by his glance, his voice, and the hands that seemed to move randomly when he was under intense scrutiny.

Knowing that I could never fully understand his history, I simply sat and listened. He was not complaining about his past, just remembering it well. He remembered how life could be cruel, how he fought for recognition. Now I was not surprised he did not mention his educational accolades. First Nations people are humble, often not displaying trophies or certificates. Although he mentioned only his academic background, I could see photos of victories won on his wall.

"You know," he said gently, then continued more gruffly, "when people are walking down the road inebriated there is a reason for that. Things like that do not happen randomly."

I nodded in agreement, beginning to understand his vision. Vince was right. A builder eventually reveals what he is made of if the house stands. A builder's care, attention to detail, and ability to include extras all stand out when a house is complete. When a house is not designed well and has few extras, it looks incomplete. I began to see why he was so insistent on being qualified.

A qualified builder cares about the community, and about children sleeping through brisk winter nights. A qualified builder cares how the house looks from the street. A house always has a reason for looking the way it does; its walls mask stories untold.

Vince continued, showing me how subfloors are laid with tongue and groove plywood, and walls are built to stand straight. Confused by the tools' names, I nodded excitedly, realizing we were reaching the roof. The basic roofs they build on reserve houses are called gable roofs. Rafters are built right at the reservation, and each house and roof looks exactly the same.

*H clips are to be on every joist?* I think he said. Leafing through his book, I tried to keep up with his explanations. H clips allow for expansion and contraction so that the plywood does not buckle. Before laying asphalt shingle, there must be a row of waterproof membrane on the edge of the sheeting. Then there can be a starter strip of shingles.

Sensing that he was losing me, he recaptured my attention with his pen. "This is where your devious friend comes in," he chided. "Without waterproofing, humidity gets into the walls and is not discovered until black spots appear on the kitchen ceiling. Or if a plumber has done a poor job and there is leakage, water seeps into the basement."

*Yuck, black spots on the roof because a journeyman cut costs,* I mused. *If the residents spent five hundred dollars on a dehumidifier, they could combat the damage – but why not just do the job properly from the start?*

"I walked off a job up north on the reserve once," he said. "The supervisor insisted we use old plywood from setting the concrete for the subflooring of the teachers' residences. He insisted that chiefs and council would never know. I did not care about that," he said, "I cared about the safety of the teachers!"

Vince is a man of integrity, teaching young students to value those same principles. House buyers should be aware of all the details when purchasing a home, to ensure that builders share that same integrity. His persistence ensures that his students build with excellence and value the difference between a house and a home.

"Houses take a couple of years to build?" I asked, once again showing my ignorance. I was open and honest, admitting I really had just purchased my first screwdriver a few years ago. He chuckled, saying he was proud of his female students who had done well in the journeyman program.

"I am a writer," I reminded him, "that is why I date men who own tools."

He laughed heartily as I sipped the remainder of my cooling coffee. Watching his expression, I could see his wisdom. My generation was more concerned with the profit of a house sale, then building a home. When our houses are unlivable, or inconvenient, they are left abandoned. The pressure to succumb to modern materialism, weakens my own strength to stand with convictions. Unsure if I would have walked off the job as Vince did, my mood sobered. *Courage is required to build a home right; even more is needed, to rebuild my broken heart that is damaged.* I thought.

"It is not about the time a house takes to be built, but about the precision taken to build it," he said.

My eyes had begun to gloss over but I knew this conversation had changed my perception of Aboriginal tradesmen. He was not qualified simply because he had gone back to school while supporting a family. He was not qualified simply because he had sacrificed and endured racial prejudice. He was not qualified simply because he refused to quit, while few believed in him. He was not qualified simply because he had a wife and family who cared deeply about him. He was not qualified simply because he consistently showed up for work and got the job done.

He was qualified because, when he built a house, he built the home, right.

## Chapter Two

# Giving is Better

# Sacrifice

My mother hung the cardboard sign around my neck, informing hospital administrators that her child needed groceries. I was promised an ice cream by the nurses' union when I was done picketing, enough to inspire a five-year old to political activism.

When I was a toddler, my mother had learned the frustration of making ends meet after divorce. Now, she refused to let us suffer from the lack of heat in our townhouse in Calgary's river district. Her graduation from nursing college and move to Alberta was supposed to improve our social status. Instead, my sister and I watched her struggle to listen to our stories after night-shift. Escaping poverty was a slow process.

When I was young, nurses were not paid well, and women earned less than men – whether or not their children were hungry. My mother did not complain; she just worked harder. We children simply became accustomed to the fact that her supervisors were more acquainted with her than we were. Accepting ever more shifts, she clung to our photos in her wallet. She was working for us, at last earning a wage that surpassed her pre-college days. After those draining 12-hour shifts, she collapsed overnight on the couch, too exhausted to plod up the stairs to her dilapidated bed. In mid-evening, I would creep quietly into her makeshift bedroom to cover her with a blanket, seeing the purple bags beneath her eyes. We satisfied ourselves with random conversations while she sipped her morning coffee. As my sister and I quietly tiptoed throughout the day, my mother felt faint optimism that her sacrifice was worthwhile.

She offered charity for those around her in our impoverished neighbourhood, despite her low income. My mother remembered what it was like to walk with children for an hour in minus thirty-degree winters because we had no vehicle. During those frigid walks, she cajoled us with smiles and songs – as though we were on an unstoppable, exciting adventure. It was so cold, my feet numbed after the first 20 minutes, but I did not have the nerve to argue. I did not always sing each time, but she always did.

Throughout the difficult college years, never do I recall her crying. Her gentle eyes seemed always to smile. She was a survivor, proactive with food costs and bills. I recall walking around the neighbourhood, singing cheerfully and asking strangers for refundable bottles. Collecting bottles paid for my skating lessons – and a little jelly candy. We cleaned yards in the spring, and delivered newspapers to buy milk at school during lunch hour. My mother planted a garden in our backyard similar to my grandparents. As I was buzzed about the house, I often heard the soft, entrancing strains of my mother's hymn-singing. While she, seemingly non-stop, punched down fresh loaves of bread or peeled beets for canning seemingly non-stop, I admired her diligence. We valued her days off, basking in her attention. Her gentle promises that one day things would be different gave us hope. One day, she said, we would spend summers camping near Athabasca Lake, mystical

Northern Lights dancing as we nestled into our tents near the campfire.

Gazing out the window, she steadily kneaded bread dough. Noticing me standing on tiptoe to see what she was looking at, she asked me to sprinkle flour on the counter and lured me into singing with her. I loved singing, and I loved how her eyes sparkled when she taught me those old hymns. She believed every lyric, and harmonized despite my loud out of tune voice. Her joy was contagious, her optimism was real. Eventually her wage did increase. We moved to a duplex on a hill overlooking the river in a small Albertan town.

## Hospitality

Finally with enough to eat ourselves, I was perplexed by her invitations to strangers for lunch after church. She woke early Sunday mornings to put a roast in the oven, measuring out the last of the flour for buns and apple pie even before dawn welcomed the day. Her meals honoured these impoverished strangers. We spent all summer measuring out sugar for our jam, and even let her convince us that weeding in the garden was fun. We knew it was not so, but looked forward to the pickled beets that would grace our Thanksgiving table. Still, we were not as eager to share as our mother.

Mother looked dishevelled at the church service after working so hard each morning, but her servant's heart shone like expensive jewels. After each service, she hugged new faces and invited old ones as though it were the first time they had dined with her. There were gentle elderly widows looking for company after a lonely week. She reached out to the struggling single mothers who had not known how they would feed their children that day. She hid a loaf of bread in the freezer to send home with them when no one else was watching. Couples and elderly widows sipped Earl Grey tea and related amusing stories to the children sitting at their feet.

The women recounted with delight the days they received only an unwrapped doll for Christmas, for which they were thankful. They recalled how the community worked together, helping neighbours during harvest. Even in the Dirty Thirties when the farmers farmed nothing but dust, they dreamed of owning a house someday. As the children played with my toys, I listened skceptically from a distance. Each visitor enjoyed the fellowship and the meal prepared with unselfish love. My mother's bread warmed their hearts like soft summer sun at the lakefront.

My sister and I spent our day making Ukrainian perogies like Baba taught us, rolling out the dough on the kitchen table, scooping potato and cheddar filling with a small teaspoon, delicately pinching edges to prevent leakage while they boiled and later fried in butter and onions. We had spent many mornings learning to knead dough and roll balls perfectly so that our buns would rise like the smile on a child's face when he saw them on the table, butter bowl nearby. Mother allowed scruffy guest children with dirty hands as much butter as they wanted. Ignoring my scowl, she opened a jar of strawberry preserves. These children had not learned to value our garden, yet my mother opened our meagre stores and welcomed the town's undesirables into our home.

In my naivety, I demanded to know why she gave others the garden beets we had pickled. She replied to my objections with the same softly spoken words, "No one should be alone at Sunday dinner."

"Can they not eat at their own home?" I argued, stomping my foot. She smiled, gently replying, "The Lord's mercies are new every morning, Paula. Great is His faithfulness."

One morning my mother returned to our dilapidated townhouse from work with tears in her eyes. Our neighbours a couple of houses down had a house fire. Her lips trembled and I thought of the little girl who played alone in the park. She had stood in the cold, tears running down her checks as she watched her home engulfed by flames of destruction. Warm tears continued to well up in my mother's beautiful brown eyes, as she explained that we needed to care. We must show that caring by going to our rooms to collect some of our clothing for our neighbours.

Reluctantly, I marched up the stairs. Slowly I placed toys into a garbage bag, as though preparing for a funeral. I was not eager to give charitably and anonymously to these traumatized children. If they were going to have my paper dolls, I should be skipped a grade by my elementary school for selflessly caring. I was more disappointed in giving up my newest games than by the children's serious loss. I really loved the soft, dusty rose, fuzzy sweaters knitted by my grandmother, and I was attached to the dainty rag doll my father had mailed me for Christmas. Worse yet, our family was going to show that we cared without acknowledgement. My mother would drop off the items with the local organizer – without our name on the plastic bag.

By the following week, daily routine recaptured our attention. On my restless journey by school bus, I tried desperately to see out the frosted window by scratching away the ice. The only thing that made this long tiresome ride bearable was seeing the new buildings sprouting in the downtown core. I loved watching the city grow. Each day, I would gaze out to see if the sidewalks were set with unwanted initials. The bus was so glacial this morning, I clapped my hands and stomped my feet to keep the blood circulating, moaning when the minus forty air flooded the bus every time the doors opened.

I felt an unexpected jolt as we came to a halt to pick up the neighbour children who had lost their house. The little Aboriginal girl with shiny dark hair and huge, slanty charcoal eyes intrigued me. A sweet face revealed her enchanting smile, melting my heart in the unforgiving winter. I remembered her from the park where my friends and I had studiously avoided her. If she came to sit on the swings, we jumped off and climbed the monkey bars. We intentionally offended her with our song *Chocolate Baby,* chanted while throwing the ball at each other. We meant her to feel unwelcome, to be reminded that she looked different. I now wished I had asked her to join us, and shown her before the fire that I was kind, or at least taken the time to meet this mysterious girl who sat at the front of the bus, protected by the bus driver. I had not even asked her name. She was the only girl in our neighbourhood with skin darker than a tan. I thought it would be awkward to have another friend over to the house even though my mother always had baked extra rich flavoured peanut butter cookies.

When the girl hesitantly stepped up onto the bus, she was clasping one of the toys that I had unwillingly donated. Her eyes sparkled, reflecting the kindness of neighbours after losing everything. The paper doll, my toy, was her only possession after the fire ravaged her bedroom. She held the box of paper dresses like a trophy, signifying that she was important after all. She had brought her new doll to school to remind us she was a vivacious little girl who would and could survive loss.

Only then did I understand what a beautiful woman my mother was. She had spoken the truth when she said, "The Lord's mercies are new every morning." On that frosty winter day, I learned through the eyes of childhood innocence, it truly is better to give than to receive.

## Chapter Three

# Angel Dust

## The Pixie Appears

Winters are harshest on the highways. The compact car slid snakelike, as uncontrollable and dangerous as the prairies themselves. The floor heat never seemed to reach our feet fast enough. We were headed to church on a Wednesday night; the drive was almost 90 minutes long. My mother had taken a position at another reserve, this time in central Alberta. Living in the country, she commuted the 30 miles to work without regret. Rural life offered solitude, a life outside her career. Thankful my senior year of high school was approaching, I lived with her on the farm for a semester. Her zest for life enabled me to endure winter's darkness in the country. Spirit-like Northern Lights faintly danced in the sky, while prairie winds beat against my windows.

As we drove, I was nervous because collisions are common near Christmas. Once the ice grabs like the devil himself, drivers are at the mercy of fate. Farm lights occasionally flashed on unplowed back roads leading to Bedlam.

Although we were headed towards a church alive with modern music, an eerie presence hung in the air. Frost rapidly recrystallized as I continuously scraped at the windows. Black ice slowed us as my mother clenched the wheel with both hands. Ordinarily very argumentative, I required peace that evening. My mother hummed tunelessly. Sensing my unease, she began mouthing favourite psalms. "As I walk through shadow of the valley of death," she chanted quietly, "I shall fear no evil." Tonight I found no comfort in those words. Shadows of death evoked memories of senseless violence in a community consumed by hopelessness. Those shadows followed people into the light.

My mother gently warned me that a young girl my age was joining us. Ever cautious, I asked questions fervently. Shrugging, my mother explained simply that Giselle had called, asking for a ride to church. Her tiny town had only one road. To the right slumped a dilapidated bar, to the left a farmhouse. Farm vehicles had scarred the road. A fence near the worn house clattered in the wind. The car slowly turned right onto a gravel road, then left onto the driveway. Bushes hid a path; a porch peeked from behind. Distracted by the plastic-covered windows, I was uninterested in this interloper, ever leery of strangers – especially those my mother adopted. Her soft heart reached out to the needy, those shunned by society. She genuinely loved them and always saw their potential.

A pixie-like figure appeared. The frail, fearless little girl jumped into the car as if she had known us for years. Curious about our reason for such a long trip, she asked us for details about the exciting journey. Giselle made enough small talk to put our minds at ease, and then the young girl shocked me by asking about my past. She was willing to reveal anything and apparently thought others should as well. Oddly, I was neither offended nor intimidated by her interrogation. She was sweet, beautiful, chatty – and endearingly intrusive.

Within the next 30 minutes, Giselle managed to

learn where I had lived over the past decade – and my favourite ice cream flavour. She nodded with empathy when I said I had lived in the East, but visited my mother in the West. Her father also lived in the East, yet she stayed with family in the West. Originally a city girl, her understanding of life on a reservation was limited.

Not even five feet tall, she was as bold as a lion. I wondered how this scrawny teenager, who probably weighed less than a hundred pounds, could possibly be so daring and engaging. Nervously fidgeting with her seatbelt, she leaned forward to ask more details about my cats. Giselle guessed that I was an animal lover, by noticing my hair covered coat. Immensely perceptive and drawn in by delightful conversation, she was ordinary yet distinctive.

Giselle largely evaded my questions about her last ten years. She was from the city and had endured enough of street life, she shrugged. I wondered at this comment, since we were the same age. Facial scars suggested otherwise.

The girl was stunningly beautiful, with high cheekbones and alluring eyes, yet weathered by life. Otherwise perfectly groomed, her hands were paper dry.

Giselle swept her long beautiful black hair to the right of her head, so that the curls flowed rhythmically around her shoulders. Although darker and of aboriginal descent, she shared many characteristics of her French ancestors. Her French father had grey hair and piercing blue eyes, she said, which explained her gravitation toward men with those attributes. Set against skin paler than other Aboriginal people and thick eyebrows framing her coal like eyes, her delicate lips rarely revealed her mesmerizing smile.

The way her leather coat elegantly draped around her small frame, she reminded me of a Persian queen. She swaggered confidently through the snow, occasionally skipping when excited. Giselle talked like a survivor, saying we would meet up one day to reminisce about our victories, reminiscing of life's battles fought valiantly.

During that semester, I learned she was shy, yet deeply interested in others. Laughing, she bounced to the car like a kangaroo when she had good news to share. We had barely met each other, but quickly became fast friends during those cold winter evenings. She knew how to make me giggle like a child, touching my heart through my tough exterior. Giselle had a way of enjoying the simplicity of life, cherishing every moment.

When faced with too many questions at once, she pensively scratched her head, and gazed at her long nails before regrooming them. She always paused, scratching her head, in order to speak persuasively. Speaking methodically, she was quick to admit she did not have solutions for every problem. Giselle dismantled firm arguments, yet built up her debate opponent. She was brave enough to speak her mind, yet kind enough to wrap each word with concern. Planning ahead, she arranged for my mother to bring her the following Wednesday as well.

Like the prairie wind, she blew through town, causing a stir, then left behind a surreal calm when her assignment and mission were done. It never occurred to me that rootless wild flowers also blow away with the wind. As she detailed all the places she had been, I knew she would not stay in her little town. Although uncomfortable with her frankness, I wanted her to stay. I wanted the winds to stop howling, to leave this new friend by my side. Occasionally I would catch her staring out the window into space, a lost little girl. Naively I shrugged away those moments, surmising that we all had brief moments of hopelessness.

She came from a broken home, and soon found herself turning tricks in the city. Now those street smarts seemed to interfere with her simple life in the small prairie town where the moon poked through the clouds each night. She seemed to fear hazy skies, dreading the clear northern lights floating over the Canadian North. When the stillness of night crept in, her gaze became more pensive, hiding thoughts that only a priest might understand. Giselle's eyes squinted; haunted by visions of a past that very few would want to remember, her body tensed at the overpowering memories. I sensed a demonic presence nearby, as though we were being watched.

## Hope

The following semester, she moved into our condominium to finish her senior year of high school. Often, a warm wind would wrap around my ankles as I approached her room. Sometimes I would jump up from the couch, thinking she was home, but the footsteps I heard were not hers. I surveyed her room, hoping to hear her humming and seeing her flipping through her favourite magazines. Instead, I saw only a neatly made bed and precisely placed belongings on her dresser. Someone or something was marking his territory, trying to tell us she did not belong in our home. I began to keep the light in the bathroom switched on during the night, hoping to catch its shadow. Her answers became defensive as though I was interrogating her. She felt the presence too, but remained quiet, perhaps to appease him.

Keeping conversation light at the supper table, we reminded each other how we only had to finish grade twelve in Alberta. We had almost graduated, and would soon be able to adventure to other nations with a duffel bag and a dream. She prepared for community college. I cajoled her to attend university, but she kept her plans to herself. She would occasionally reveal secrets – like her passion for home design. We argued over the latest project that compelled her to take apart her jackets, even though she was not experienced enough to resew them. Pinning together a jacket with a safety pin, she proved that her design had merit.

Sometimes, to avoid sleeping, she would keep me awake, explaining how she was going to be a famous designer some day. One day while watching television, she said I would someday see her showing her latest line. Seeing how cleverly she fixed our hair and makeup, I believed her.

She flipped through magazines and ate ice cream as if it was free. A natural money-maker and the proud owner of a calculator, she was fascinated by news clips that analyzed the economy. She spoke of economic programs introduced by the government and non-profit organizations, knowing I would be enticed into the discussion. Routinely shocked by her political insight at just seventeen, I listened intently as though she were a bank manager laying out my financial future. She offered practical solutions for the common investor, reminding me regularly that facial expressions are often a good indicator of how people are doing. Those experiencing the consequences of decisions made for them reveal what kind of leadership we have at a national level. Insisting that Aboriginal people are expressionless and therefore not good indicators of the political climate, she paused in her usual way. She wanted to explain her role in society, without my passionate debate. As teenagers, we could reason, but we did not yet understand our role in the community.

## The Rescuer

With pithy lectures that bored even me, I scolded her that negligence was the reason for her poor marks. She had immense potential, if she only trained her mind to become more disciplined and focused. I wasn't convinced that the design world would bring her riches. After all, few people in small towns hired designers. While living on the street, she had overcome the cocaine addiction that affected her ability to succeed academically. The after effects still interfered with her abilities.

I did not understand how a chemical could break her will. Surely, I thought, if she just focused, Giselle could graduate from any program she chose. She was now free of dependence on drugs, yet still tortured from the long reaching effects of an all but forgotten past. She could not easily retain information, and even had to be reminded of appointments. I did not want to believe that a teenager with her potential could possibly be so pillaged by Angel Dust. I could not grasp how a powder could render this dynamo powerless.

Those with little self-control used drugs, in my youthful opinion. I militantly assured her that if only she would try harder, she would beat the cycle. I convinced her that goal setting develops inner strength, that self-empowerment overcomes despair and disappointment. I had never known the fear of abandonment or the paralyzing nausea of a man's drunken breath on my skin. I had never known the lustful touch of a married man seeking sexual release with a stranger.

Substance abuse erased the sting, she said. Sexual trade was a neutral business transaction; it had nothing to do with intimacy. I shivered as she described how men of every religion push their ties to the side and enter women they consider of no value. Unable to withstand the tormenting images, I tried to lighten the mood with casual conversation. Seeing my ignorance and desperate for my compassion, she revealed why she loved the drug, even though she no longer used it.

The drug allowed her to forget about the streets, the years she was friendless, and a time in her life when she could read a book all the way through. She spoke of Angel Dust like some angelic euphoria - like heavenly songs. She spoke of it longingly, caring more for Angel Dust than for the God who punished her for being nameless.

I had no compassion for an addict, nor did I want to hear more stories that took away my respect. Life on the street can be a tough, dirty existence. Drug addicts living there only remind society why we need law enforcement. As long as she was clean now, sleeping in a real bed, I could remain indifferent to the street dwellers' lives of disappointment. I did not want her to remind me that so many Aboriginal youths are lost and never found.

I shushed her, hoping to minimize the stories so we could continue our carefree reading. I wanted her to sleep well at night, to be thankful for a clean bed and food. The past was finished, I said, a past nightmare. I had poor advice for someone so consumed by emotional wounds. Impatience for the time that healing takes dripped from my soul like blood from a wound. I would only applaud her accomplishments, awarding smiles of adoration when she redirected her life toward middle class morality. It was a misguided concept - expecting middle class achievements to purify evil. Education would remove the stain of blood, I insisted. She would have a home, children and more opinions about upcoming elections. She would smile again, sipping tea while reading her favourite books as neighbours looked on approvingly.

I wanted to transform her - to wear designer jeans, hang out at the cafe without recognizing her johns, and joke around like teenagers should. Then the phone rang late one night. I was so exhausted, I thought it was my alarm clock. I rubbed my fatigued eyes and lifted up the telephone receiver.

## Dark Nights

"Paula," a sheepish, yet highly intoxicated voice slurred.

"Why are you calling?" I growled.

"I need a ride home," she blurted.

"I am not rescuing you," I snarled. I refused to encourage this behaviour. A lonely walk in the cool night air might act as a catalyst for sobriety.

"*I need you,*" she whispered, with the voice of a trapped animal. It was the voice of a lost child, buried beneath her debating, stubborn resilience. It was the voice of innocence lost, of tearful regret. I could not leave her to freeze. She would probably stagger home, fall, and end up a tragedy in the newspaper.

"Just stay where you are. Stay on the corner," I relented, "so I can find you."

Even though I felt like jailing her myself, I knew no one would rescue her, like those forgotten teens waiting near the mall to bum change for coffee. So many times I had searched for her until it frightened and frustrated me, robbing me of hope. Now revenge oozed through my mind, even as grief overwhelmed me. As the tears ran down my cheeks, I begged God to rescue her. If she died that evening, my heart would shatter.

As I wandered down the empty streets, I found her standing fearlessly on the corner. She wore her favourite black jogging pants and leather jacket. Noticing how at home she felt on the street, my heart sank. Still, my frustration made me abrupt. "Get your ass into the car," I said. Sighing with relief as she snuggled into the warmth of the car, she enthusiastically expressed her gratitude. I retorted that silence was preferable, but nothing would spoil her mood. Highly annoyed, I became even more vexed when police lights flashed behind us. Assuming I was inebriated, the officer asked me to step out of the car. I assured him I was sober, then imploring, "Really officer, I do not mind if you want to book her."

Giselle's off-key singing filled the cruiser as the officer checked my plates. Returning, he suggested I take her home. I felt betrayed by the one man trusted to keep peace in our town. Police are not paid to baby-sit drunks; they are hired to arrest criminals. His grimace told me he had listened to enough off-key singing for one night. She just needed a good rest and a couple of counselling sessions, I said. I took her home, knowing that everyone else had given up on her. In the morning, classical music would be my revenge.

Sobriety became worse than drunkenness as she wrestled demons from her past, and struggled with new relationships. Fearful once the sun went down, she purposely found ways to stay awake. I again began to feel the dark presence waiting for her. I was just a spectator, hearing her quietly whimper as nightmares ravaged her sleep. Hoping that music would calm her, each night I played psalms like the ones my mother had sung.

At my suggestion, Giselle purchased holy oil, trying to help herself as well as she could. She desperately wanted to be free, to dance in the moonlight as she had in the summer sun. We continued to lose ground.

*How can I watch a friend who is helpless?* I prayed, asking for strength.

The white dust lured her – an immediate solution for loneliness. Angel Dust reinspired the artist, releasing wings to flutter again, but it was an enemy that left casualties. Even when she was sober, it tortured Giselle with flashbacks and unresolved pain. Thinking I was asleep, she slipped into my room as the moon rose in the sky, curling up, a puppy at my feet, then vanishing before I woke. If prevention is better than cure, then she would need to sleep like a child.

I lay there while she slept, watching the peace that came over her face as I covered her with my extra blanket. *What kind of demon could provoke a lost young girl to sleep like a dog at my feet?* I wondered.

I lay awake, feeling as though I failed her. I prayed that God would have mercy on her, that she would no longer need me to protect her one day. Band-Aid solutions would not suffice, and she would have to leave eventually. Angel Dust takes no prisoners, heals no wounds. Even when the dust is no longer being snorted, the damage lingers. Money is no longer wasted on this imaginary friend, only sleepless nights.

Struggling to heal her wounds, my own grew. I felt helpless, haunted by nightmares and walking on eggshells to avoid her latest mood swing. Life became unbearable. There seemed to be no restoration for this broken heart, only rehab where teens were sent to be confronted by unforgiving parents. Coming from a broken home, I knew I could easily have struggled with the same addiction. Dust would weaken me as quickly as it did her. I read self-help books in the hope that some well-educated counsellor would reassure me these problems only happened to Aboriginal youth – I need not fear my own weaknesses. Each night as the hours ticked by, I wondered when she returned if would she shut me out of that world of disenchantment she had seduced me into.

I was giving up, knowing I had failed, and wanting to distance myself from even the memory of this girl I had once believed in. Like an unpaid counsellor, my time and energy had been spent on her. I left to find a home where I would never again encounter that pain and disappointment.

While I attended college, Giselle remained, consumed by her fight for a clear mind. The wind did blow, and we both danced free of roots in the prairie soil, but

I had been too callous to hear her feelings when she struggled to reveal them. Impulsively, she chose to go with a heart that often lied.

I knew I could forget my past and achieve my academic goals. In my own apartment, I could forget the winters rescuing Giselle; forget her sleeping peacefully at the end of my bed. She became a fading memory, which was often awakened at funerals.

Years later, when I heard she was back on the streets, I dropped to my knees and wept. I had stopped looking for her; now she was lost. As friends described *that girl* to me, I knew they were talking about Giselle. I stopped their bantering, reminding them she had a name - a beautiful name — and once, a hopeful future. Somewhere she lost sight of that during her sleepless nights, only at peace when she curled up like a puppy at my feet. She was a pixie, enchanting us all, chained by a force not her own.

She would have to find herself now, I knew, but I am still looking. Every night I stare out my frosty window hoping that Giselle will come home.

## Chapter Four

# Good Morning Glory

## Learning to Trust

In a small prairie town, you can watch your dog get lost for three days. I felt invincible in summer, dependent on no one, while I was driving up and down the five-minute-long main street. When I popped in at the local truck stop, my high school friends were debating *heavy metal* bands. *Which is worse?* In our town, there were teens who had money for gasoline and those who did not have. My friends were at the pit, which proved they had a car, making us the *haves.* Being a *have* was better than being a *have not* (like the Aboriginal people on the reserve outside of town). Rumour spread that they had lots of "oil royalties" coming to their people; the teenagers all owned brand new cars. With dust permanently embedded in the floorboards, and broken windows from gravel stones that were never going to be fixed, they drove off the reserve and into the neighbouring small towns *looking for trouble.*

Nobody trusted these out-of-towners because they were dark skinned, and, in their opinion, were either going to start a fight or be in one. The only excitement our small town saw were the fights outside the bar between the young cowboys and natives stumbling out drunk, heading for their trucks. In our province, "oil towns" redefined gun control policies. Roughnecks arrived for work on the oilrigs from Germany and the

United States; these tradesmen were trying to make a living and endured high rental costs of basement suites. Small town girls worked in restaurants to save enough money for college, or catch a man's eye for marriage. The prairies made everyone a survivor, regardless of language. Locals were practical, and women wanted their men to work. Often the highway restaurants were packed with village residents keeping warm while slurping coffee, bundled in fleece jackets. Easterners quickly learned to sit and wait out a storm with the locals, receiving valuable advice such as keeping a shovel and cat litter in the trunk in case they got stuck. The seasons united the community, fuelling debates on how to keep children interested, entertained, engaged, or occupied. The only time we truly united beliefs was during the hockey strike.

*They cannot possibly want to just sit at the hockey rink, cheering on the local boys for another 40 flippin years?* I muttered, waving my glass in the air to catch the attention of the waitress. The truth was they did, and they were equally confused by my disenchantment. The small town offered so much stability, especially in the West, where practical people spoke their piece, leaving no room for vivid imaginations and thrill seeking. Cowboys rode bulls until they snapped a backbone, but the prairie girl was expected to hum like an angel. I longed to be inspired by an intelligent woman who understood me and accepted my thinking. However, I set aside my disenchantment with w*estern life* the evening my mother invited me to a church service, promising a concert. I was so desperate for something new, even gospel harmonizers drew my fancy.

Sitting reluctantly in the back of the church on uncomfortable office chairs usually reserved for late attendees, I became mesmerized by a band member who played piano while singing. *She sings like an angel*, I observed, gawking at her alluring long lashed eyes. They fluttered as she smiled, larger than life. She could not be ignored. Her mannerisms challenged the ideologies deeply embedded in our small town society. Her sweater was fuzzy and unique, complementing the blonde curls skimming her shoulders. Glory was her name, although the women kept calling her Gloria. She was so well received that people crowded around her after the concert. Listeners were enchanted by tales of the band's trip to Tennessee, the heart of Dixieland.

The canola outside smelled like eastern incense, soothing the senses and calming the nerves of hard-working rural people. Everyone was relaxed, and it was time to enjoy the sounds of country music which brought joy to the tired. Farmers gave themselves to growing crops in an unforgiving land. Waiting out the winter, they dreamed of spring when the land must be prepared. Always a leap of faith to run a farm with all of the challenges, they learned to appreciate the simple things, because worry only produces fear. Many of the older farmers clapped their hands to the beat, occasionally shuffling boots as the rhythm changed. Gazing about the room, I appreciated their time of celebration. I was intrigued how this girl from the farm lived in a tour bus, not missing home like most young ladies. Her eyes merely looked towards the next destination, and wondered how she was free.

I asked for her address and how she survived with a band on the road. She grinned broadly, explaining she was the fourth youngest of a family of 15. "Feeding that many children, makes a mother and her helpers learn to creatively problem solve." She had learned to appreciate her family and to live with personalities different from her own. *Middle child syndrome* made this soft-spoken girl a natural candidate for attention seeking. Unable to sit quietly, she could always be heard in another room humming or finishing someone's sentence. She seemed to enjoy a verbal challenge, and I was vexed by my need to keep a dictionary by the phone when she called. Glory's ambition to change the world inspired me. I longed to mend our wayward hearts. Because friendship was like trying to blend vinegar and oil, we rarely discussed our ancestral backgrounds.

Humming while she baked bread in her apartment, she bagged a loaf for me to take home. Her father was German and mother Aboriginal, yet they had raised her more culturally refined than I had been. She understood the value of homemade cheesecakes and tortes at a dinner party, and appreciated delicately painted bone china placed before a stranger. I would touch and soothingly "oooh," but questioned its relevance in the mid afternoon. After we had left the proper homes of our acquaintances or the specialty cafés, Glory would often remind me that china creates an ambience. She assured me that the dainty teacups reminded artisans to appreciate humanity's fragility. She had her own experiences with abusive people, a kindred spirit who offered me solace.

While I was away at college, my mother telephoned to say Glory now had a daughter. Naturally, *band life* was not good for a new single mother. As she was buffeted by a tornado of misjudgements, she remained certain each challenge was conquerable. She was not only a confidante when I returned west, but my reason for change—a survivor of the unfair consequences life had rendered unjustly. My experiences with First Nations people had left me a realist, and I was now seen as a rebel dressed in black; *a seer* shunned for uninvited investigations, denied access by the rude enforcers. Rarely did I fit in. Nor was I able to ignore people in the community on their *third chance to get things right.* Even while my own thoughts isolated me, I found Glory's honesty engaging.

Glory reminded me of the importance of being courageous enough to celebrate, a skill learned from the older farmers, as they listened to her music. Perhaps the rhythm and flow of life was too much for dreamers. That is why Glory tried even harder to live for the moment. She often reminded me to rejoice because opposing fear will break contention. She knew I struggled with the simplicity of joy. Racism could not quash her smile. As a Métis, she understood how differences could isolate people; she valued acceptance and healing.

I sometimes felt almost indignant, as though I were trapped in the prairies for life. I yearned to escape, never to return home. Glory, fearless traveller, made me jealous. My curtains were drawn, jeans and T-shirts still black. I asked her quietly how she could smile so widely. I asked how she as a single mother, who had been looked down upon because of where she came from, could sit at a piano and celebrate? Shyly and methodically, she reminded me that she was free. Freedom from an unjust past is a powerful catalyst for a smile. As she rocked her child to sleep at night, softly humming to calm her daughter, she had become desperate for a God who was real. "The past," she explained, "is not erased by an agency or a cheque. Real joy comes from being free after winning small victories—like buying new shoes because there is enough money at the end of the month." I was vaguely happy that she blossomed in the city, but I secretly hated her for being so courageous.

Knowing my own failed relationships, I knew that public humility because of a cowardly lover is debilitating. Left a victim, she aspired to be a hero. I despised her desire to be healed and move on. All my running had left me attached to no one. Her past robbed her of sleep at night as mine did, yet she refused to become jaded toward love or marriage. Men had failed her like they had me, yet she entered university, intent on creating a better life for her child. She gladly embraced every opportunity. One day she would meet a fearless man who would be a loving father for her child. Hope consumed her, refocusing her plans.

As we flitted through academia, we quickly learned to use our voices and enjoyed hearing ourselves think. As both student and single mom, Glory had very little time, yet she arrived faithfully for lunch at my apartment. I enjoyed her company and she enjoyed a free meal. We often laughed until tears rolled down our cheeks as we dunked freshly spiced foccacia bread in olive oil and balsamic vinegar. Following years of experience in professional cooking, I had mastered recipes that spoke to the heart and calmed the nervous. Although in a Métis program with small classes that allowed her to shine, she was often conflicted. It was a challenge to live by those cultural expectations of the Métis people that contrasted with her role in the white community. She was white-skinned, her hair blonde. Often weary while seeking refuge at my kitchen table, she questioned her intelligence. She wondered if her program was designed to wean Aboriginals off welfare, instead of teaching them real skills. Glory did not want to be set up for failure.

After repeated reassurances, she would eventually collapse on my tattered couch to stroke my kitten, Josephine, the wrong way so that her fur would protrude and her whiskers would twitch. Although Glory had smouldering eyes and a smile that would melt an angry man's heart, she was an antagonist; insisting to Josephine, a snarly, domestic cat bent on being antisocial, that she was in my life and permanently. They reconciled. The only friend with whom I would enjoy a good debate also battled wits with a cat. Josephine would back up towards her slowly, mewing weak apologies and hints to be petted just one more time. Glory often had that effect on those around her, they would almost always need to come back in the most awkward way.

Glory and I had been good friends for so long that we could keep our friendship rich and deep regardless of geographical separation. Her Métis upbringing made her a natural nomad. She moved often, abandoning me to face the life I wanted to escape. As I put down roots in Saskatoon, she visited. Accustomed to her culture, I learned to enjoy her in the moment. Many First Nations people have their own sense of time. They live in the now, rarely thinking of the future, which is why they are confused by our European disenchantment with this truancy. Only adaptable people truly appreciate this facet of Aboriginal culture. After living on the reserves myself, and having grown up with only one clock in the house, her complete loss of time did not faze me. Glory simply finished a project when the time was right for her, and came to visit when she was needed.

One morning, after she had stayed the week, I asked since her appointments with the Métis society were done, would she bake some cinnamon buns? Glory's mother was one of those Aboriginal women locally famous for her baking, and had taught her daughter the secrets of cinnamon. I lingered for hours over the thought of coming home to freshly baked cinnamon buns. Concentrating on socio-economic policy during my class at university became difficult, because my stomach growled and my mind danced with visions of her masterpiece. While searching through my kitchen that morning, she indicated that I had very few ingredients, making it difficult to produce her usual high quality. Knowing my demanding personality, she reluctantly agreed to have delicious cinnamon buns ready upon my return.

After fifteen minutes of enduring winter air scratching my face that made me regret attending class, I raced through the door, a child anticipating Christmas – buns perfectly swirled, dusted lightly with just enough cinnamon. The treats were as professional as any pastry chef could attain. I was delighted and adored the cinnamon buns, yet they lacked white icing. The color seemed dark, they were beautiful and yet something was just not right. Being a professional cook and problem solver, I needed to offer help. I ran to the corner store to buy some cream cheese for icing. I was delighted with myself; I had offered a win-win solution—as the corporate community says. Returning home I was surprised by Glory's saddened face and swollen eyes.

Shocked, I stammered, yet inherently understood that this was not a simple issue. Handing her a tissue, I emphatically explained it was not about her baking, I just wanted a little extra for the cinnamon buns. I was at a loss as to why something functional had become emotional. To me cooking was a job. The buns just needed to be sweeter and have some icing on top to complement the expensive dark roast coffee I had splurged on for her. My attempts to explain were weak, and her eyes remained swollen the rest of her stay.

Cooking was indeed a job, and her way of thanking me for a bed; but the buns were only part of the expression of that thank you. In fact, it took nine years for me to understand. To me, the final and perfect product had meant more than the relationship she offered. Glory was a good friend as long as she looked right, as long as she produced tangible products society could gloat over. Generations before me had done the same thing to her people. As long as there was white icing covering the baking, the baking tasted marvellous.

I did not just lose the enjoyment of a dessert that evening; I lost a piece of my conscience. I began to realize that she was free, wanting to bake for me because she was thankful, and sing for me because she had a song. It was I who refused to celebrate.

A mosaic of culture did not need blending. She was marvellous with or without the extra sweetness of icing. She, like the blossoms of a morning glory, warmed the heart and healed the broken. A beautiful flower grew outside my back door, waiting to be appreciated. I did not comprehend that through my selfish demands I would one day wake with regret. My cultural ignorance had left her feeling unwelcome in my home. I lost the delightful aroma of my *Morning Glory*.

Our friendship stretched the following year when she moved permanently to the city. Despite our busy schedules, we found time to meet at lunch, talking openly about our different perspectives. Smiling through our conversation, I knew that she wanted to reveal a secret. Like a captured spy, at my prodding she blurted out that she had received flowers from BLUE.

"Get out?" I snorted, "The man from North Carolina?"

My heart raced, fearful for her. Internet dating was still deemed suspicious, especially with men from different countries. Wanting to protect her child and my best friend, I began to investigate. I insisted she give me the website, so that I could interrogate him anonymously. Enrolling under an assumed name, I spied on this man named BLUE to ensure he was not cheating on her with five other cyber-hussies. On the contrary, he was a journalist who adored how her femininity and independence delicately intertwined, a single man impressed with her achievements and dedication to making a better life for her daughter. He yearned to be a father, and was happy to hear that hers was out of the picture. Thinking that was odd, it occurred to me that he simply wanted to be the father.

Glory blushed as she described him to me.

"What were his emails like?"

"Ohhhh . . ."

I sighed, "It sounds like you got mail!"

When my fears subsided, she dripped out every detail, and oozed over his morning phone calls to wish her well and pray for her. Every evening, he would call to say goodnight. He was wishing her good morning, because he wanted her to experience the difference between dating and old fashioned courting. Pursuing a woman who intoxicated him required gentleman-like behaviour. It seemed so ironic, that my friend, who prided herself on flirtatious behaviour, was being scolded by a romantic writer. Each word and reassurance reminded her that he valued communication.

My grandparents had courted through letters. They only met four times before their marriage day, yet remained married fifty-five years. Romance and endurance require good communication. My grandmother cherished those letters, and spoke longingly of the days she rushed to the mailbox to see my grandfather's beautiful penmanship. He was a gentleman who believed in *forever*.

"He amused me, and intrigued me," Glory laughed. After meeting BLUE online, I believed her. They began speaking politely as friends . . . .

**6-18-01**

Good to chat with you in the chat room, today.

I'm envious that you are in western Canada. I miss the mountains of Colorado. Having dry air is so much better than the heat and humidity of North Carolina.

Drop me a line if you wish.

**6-19-01**

*Hi Blue.*

How are you today? I feel a bit like Kathleen Kelly from "You've Got Mail," right now. Are you freaked out yet? Actually, I meant it when I said platonic, and I'm glad you agreed.

I've never been to North Carolina, or Colorado for

that matter, but if it's anything like Tennessee (did I spell that right?) I know what you mean about the humidity, and all.

I'll probably send a "let's get to know each other" kind of survey, if you're interested, which is more facetious than serious. Until then, go with God.

g.l.funk
B.A. B.Ed. Student
University of Saskatchewan

Amused that she purposefully added her letters not yet attained, I was eager to see how their romance began before the beautiful flower arrangement arrived. He found her work address on the Internet, and publicly adored her, unlike her previous boyfriends. He was different; he genuinely cared for her well being. He wanted to know every facet of her personality before uttering words without meaning. They both valued a hatred for compromise, and were principled about keeping promises. Love was not a game in their early thirties, but a rare possibility.

**6-19-01**

*Hello,*

As I, too, have seen the movie, shall I call you Kathleen? How about "shopgirl?" Maybe we can start our missives with: "Dear Friend." Maybe you can tell me about butterflies in the subway and I can tell you about flour fogs on a New York street. There are no flour fogs here, though. Mosquito fogs, yes.

Yes, platonic is good. I think with all the needy and lonely people out there in chatland, I need to officially and legally change my name to platonic. Being too friendly in the Net has its disadvantages. I am glad we're on the same wavelength.

The problem with the humidity in North Carolina is that when it's really hot and humid, the bugs are out in force. You can almost convince yourself that you are a walking piece of flypaper. Ewwww!

My native Colorado can get hot in the summer, but there always are places you can go for some relief. Not here in eastern N.C. There is no escape.

Tell me, how long have you been going to chatrooms? What was it that compelled you to go? Meetchristians.com is a real good chatroom I have found in my four days of being a chatter. Christianchat has its quirks. Lots of teens in the singles room. Lots of people who also want to privately chat. Yesterday I told several just to hang out on the board and chat away. Someone named Brooke liked that idea.

Tell me about the city/town in which you live. I'd enjoy the survey. Oh, and a little facetiousness is a good thing.

Bill

**6-20-01**

*Hi, Blue*

Feel free to call me "shopgirl" and I'll call you "NY152" and do tell me about flour fogs because I'm sure to see a butterfly soon on my local city transit. Though I have to disagree, hats are a very good investment when one is running late to work and hasn't time to style hair appropriately.

I'm glad you agree that platonic is good. This past year I lived through (vicariously) the potential horrors of chatroom romances with my older sister. It took her all the way to Ontario to meet up with a 24-year old 7-11 employee who was living out of a shoebox, and tore her family apart. I didn't get into ChristianChat on purpose, I was simply curious and I'm happy to have met you and others in this way. I will not give out my e-mail freely, as you might have guessed, and I sensed something in your tone that could be trusted. I'll leave it at that.

Enjoy the survey and feel free to get creative with your responses. I'll come up with a sequel, sometime.

P.S. Crushed stinkweed works well as insect repellent, if you don't mind repelling every living thing as well.

## *SURVEY FOR THE VAGUELY CURIOUS TYPES*

1. NAME OR PSEUDONYM IF PREFERRED: Glory L. Funk a.k.a. glory838
2. AGE OR CLOSEST APPROXIMATE (HINT: ROUND DOWN TO THE NEAREST FIFTH): 30
3. GENDER, IF KNOWN: female
4. OCCUPATION (PAID, VOLUNTEER, SLOTH): student, childcare worker, worship leader
5. HEIGHT (WITHOUT ELEVATED FOOTWEAR UNLESS THAT'D EMBARRASS YOU): 5'5"
6. LITERACY LEVEL (COLLEGE LEVEL, SOMEONE IS HELPING YOU WITH THIS SURVEY): senior university level (I enjoy reading the dictionary)
7. LINGUISTICS (ARTICULATE OR STILL

GRUNTING): my best friend Paula needs a dictionary when we're talking

8. POSSESSION OF COMMON SENSE (STRONG OR YOU CAN'T CHANGE A LIGHT BULB IF THE FATE OF YOUR FIRST-BORN DEPENDED ON IT): strong (I do my own home repair)
9. AUTO LICENCE (TRUCKER, BASIC AUTO DRIVER, ONLY DURING DAYLIGHT HOURS, ONLY WITHIN A 5M RADIUS OF YOUR TOWNSHIP): basic auto driver
10. AVERAGE HOURS OF SLEEP PER NIGHT: 7.5
11. AVERAGE DESIRED HOURS OF SLEEP PER NIGHT: 6 (I'd get a lot more accomplished if that's all I needed)
12. TYPICAL DREAM SEQUENCE (YOU DREAM ABOUT WORK OFTEN, HEDONISTIC, AGGRESSIVE COMBAT, YOUR DREAMS WOULD SCARE A CHAINSAW MURDERER): my dreams border on hedonistic but I would say they are mostly pure and pleasant
13. FAVORITE ICE CREAM, SORBET, FROZEN YOGURT: espresso flake or mocha (can we say java addict?)
14. YOUR LAUGH CLOSELY RESEMBLES THAT OF SANTA CLAUS, CINDERELLA'S MICE, THE COUNT ON SESAME STREET: I laugh a bit like Meg Ryan
15. MUSICAL ABILITIES (BONA FIDE, PLEASE - KAZOOS ARE PARTY FAVORS

Oh I laughed, that is my best friend. She was notorious for her attention to detail and intelligence gathering. I wanted so desperately for this wonderful friend to meet the husband she dreamt of. He was a man who not only believed in old fashioned courting, but in fatherhood. Statistically, single moms do not find love. Yet here were two thirty-somethings overcoming statistics. They had wrestled with their demons of the past, and embraced their future. Transcending cultural differences, they formed a respectable friendship. He took interest in her daughter's ballet lessons, and how she curled her hair each day. When Blue sent her daughter a book to engage her mind, I knew that he was Glory's soul mate, even though she was still sceptical. He emailed me right away, asking me to be honest about our friendship and who she was. I could say very little that was negative, and suggested that she was a friend who healed the broken hearted. She believed the best of her family, although they discouraged her sympathy. She was dear, and I wished her happiness. I knew that she was eager to have a family, and that her hope would not be disappointed.

**7-3-01 (5:30 p.m.)**

*Hi there, Glory. :)*

Blue is sad that you can't chat. :(

Well, although they are slower, e-mails and letters are in many ways better. You will just have to sedate me while I am waiting for your responses. :)

I am distraught that you have an aversion to cats. They are so fluffy and furry. They purr and crawl in your lap. Then they knead their little sharp claws into your skin, and, and, uh, they scratch and claw and, and, they, uh, shed and... You know, actually, I hate cats.

What was I thinking? And I wouldn't want you to turn into a drug dealer who hates being one, so the felines will have to go.

How about gerbils?

I have to admit to being extremely excited, thrilled, intrigued and curious about getting to know you. I just may have to get a second job so I can pay my phone bill, but it would be worth it. Once you hear someone's voice, the chats and the e-mails don't quite do it. What do you think? (I'm hearing you say, "ya think?")

Work goes in spurts here. I have phone calls to make and interviews to conduct, but there is some lull time here and there during the day. Most of the afternoon I was out of the office interviewing principals and teachers who are preparing for the beginning of year-round school that starts on Monday.

I haven't chatted all that often at work, but when I have, it's been for a few moments. My personal computer activities consist mostly of writing e-mails.

Feel free to call, too, if you can.

God bless.

Bill

**7-4-01**

*Hello, Bill*

I'm sooo tired, I can hardly stay vertical. I'm trying to say something rational, but I feel stoned and I've never even done anything more than pain relievers which were actually prescribed to a much older, much bigger CanArmy guy, and I took them by accident.

Bill, I don't know what God has in mind yet, I know how this feels to me, and I know better than to rely on my emotions as any sort of indicator of God's will for me or you. I really don't want to rush things, and I can't help holding back some of what I'm thinking or feeling. I don't want to get hurt and I don't want to hurt you either.

We've covered a lot of heavy issues in a short time and, although I know God's in control, He would have us be wise and reasonable as well. My life is too precious to make any wrong steps and so is yours. I want you to have breathing space, and I need that too, Bill. I'm not saying "no," I'm saying "slower." Please accept that from me, your friend.

Yours is Christ, Glory

Protective of her heart, he respected her honesty. They spent hours on the phone enjoying each other's company. They were friends, and, like he wrote in his emails, Glory had his full attention. When she spoke with me months later, she announced her future travels to North Carolina. He, of course, would travel to Canada first, like a gentleman. We were both nervous, even though it was her relationship. *Did old-fashioned courting, like my grandfather's, work?* The process seemed so dreamy, like a romance novel unfolding. He was not the type of man she usually dated, he even enjoyed feisty debates. *Her selection was improving!* He stimulated her mind, and respected her boundaries. Although my friends and I pointed quickly to his need to organize her, he gently offered her tips for ordering her day.

**7-5-01**

*Good morning, Glory,*

I hope you had a good rest last night and that you are wide-awake and refreshed today.

I slept for eight hours last night - the most I have slept in a long time. I also went to bed earlier than I had in quite a while. I appreciate your e-mail you sent yesterday afternoon. We're on the same page, Glory. I agree with you on going about this slowly. This definitely is not something to rush, and there is no reason to do so. Like you, I, too, wish for us to get to know one another as friends. That takes time.

With that, my friend, Glory, I wish you a blessed day.

Bill

When Blue arrived, Glory's daughter accepted this man who valued her mother. Old enough to sense genuine friendship, she embraced the respect he offered his best friend. As they slowly melded into a possible family, walking in unity that requires patience and diligence, I knew she would leave me. My heart was lonely before I helped her pack. She had found her soul mate while becoming honest with herself. She was experiencing the rewards of hope. My smile did not waiver as we loaded her last box; BLUE had earned our respect. Glory was leaving her home to build a new one, and I missed her even before she boarded the bus.

## Chapter Five

# Just Like My Baba

# Hard Lessons Learned

Retreating to my grandparents' acreage was a reprieve from city concrete. As we drove towards the cabin where they stood guard, we inhaled the fragrance of uncut wild flowers in the pasture. I would eagerly spend the warmth of summer shelling peas with my soft-spoken grandmother, listening to heart-wrenching tales of the Dirty Thirties. Her calm rural simplicity relieved the pressures of competing with college classmates. Hip to hip before the stove, she stirred delicious broth while I learned how to add just a hint of oh-Grandma-that-smells-so-good.

She peeled and sliced garden vegetables as a mealtime staple, and we ate the costly butter sparingly. Plucking cloves from the jar as if sharing a secret, she dotted eyes on dove-shaped buns baked for her kitchen helpers alone. Rich aromas wafted throughout the home. Raised a farm girl, she understood and valued the art of survival.

As pink dawn greeted our sleepy faces, Grandma was already sipping coffee, perusing proverbs from her tattered Bible. She spent hours at that table, listening to my dreams. A writer who relished storytelling, Grandma encouraged me to be creative with my humor. We giggled away the warm evenings, playing cards with Grandpa Paul, somehow knowing life is precious. After my parents' divorce, my grandparents' home became my home, Grandma an anchor in a chaotic world of custody conflicts. Her warm smile a reprieve from the rejection, she touched my soul, gently clasping my young heart in her soft hands.

Breakfast with my grandparents was well worth the tedious drive from the stress of finals, even though I had every tree memorized. In Edmonton, I met my mother for the drive to our final refuge. She had become an outpost nurse in Northern Alberta, my sophomore year. She missed me so badly that she gladly endured the radio's blaring country music and my out-of-tune accompaniment.

She took the job up north to challenge her skills, soon discovering a mystical world among First Nations people who eagerly await sunrise, read the date by the moon, and lose track of time.

My grandfather, an Air Force veteran turned pilot, believed in discipline and hard work. We all had a job to do in order to earn Grandma's canned peach dessert. I was assigned squirrel duty. If a small flower-eating rodent dared get within a ten-foot radius of Grandma's prized pink roses, I was to fire a warning shot.

To no avail, I struggled to make my grandfather understand that I was an urban girl, barely competent with a can opener. Despite a summer spent on a northern reservation, I had not learned to handle a rifle. Heck, if I brought up the subject in the downtown core back in Saskatoon, it sparked a heated gun control debate at the coffee shop. Grandpa's blank stare clearly told me he would not excused me from guard duty. Apparently, the squirrels and rabbits nibbled garden vegetables, ruined flowers, and created dangerous potholes.

My aim was hopeless. Any pellet from my weapon was just a warning shot. When the crafty varmints realized only a frightened girl was in charge, they taunted me from the edge of the flower garden. Fluffy bunnies twitched arrogant noses, beady eyes defiant. Grandpa told me inner authority is greater than outer authority. No matter how passionately I wielded my would-be weapon of destruction, it became obvious: my inner strength was not apparent to any of the four-footed intruders. Perceiving my ineptitude, other lurkers meandered closer.

The black lab, named Putin after a Russian poet, gazed at me with cocked head and laid-back ears, clearly embarrassed by my inadequacy.

To my dismay, the chubby gray ringleader condescendingly thumped his back paw, insolently shifting his weight while placidly chewing Grandma's favorite lilies. The gray devil did not even flinch when Putin yelped as my stray pellet nicked his hindquarters. The whimpering puppy took cover, scowling like a woman scorned at this shooter who did not understand the code of rural loyalty. Snarling, he wagged his jaw as if to say, "You never shoot the dog, dummy!" I had not meant to shoot Putin – the gun just seemed to fly to the left every time I fired. Meanwhile the intruders haughtily stared, as if to convey, "That's right girlfriend, shoot the dawg!"

The next day, Grandpa issued my new weapon: an old garden hose. I had been demoted to garden watering duty. Delighted by the demotion, I hummed with delight each evening as I spent hours ensuring the peas flourished under my loving care. The wounded Putin lived, which is perhaps how I came that evening to be indulged with peaches smothered in vanilla bean ice cream.

Both my grandparents insisted that my mother and I learn how food grows, so that we could fully understand the meaning of thankfulness and patience. Food did not grow on grocery store shelves, they said. Seeds were planted, weeds killed by the gardener's sweat in the hot summer sun, and patience blossomed along with each delicate leaf. Growing sufficient produce for a family's winter stores demands diligence. We weeded even when it was inconvenient, watered when it was dry. Exhausted, we were rewarded when Grandma led us into the pea patch to demonstrate how the sowing and reaping began. She detailed how seeds must be planted, how they are cared for. I was hoping someone would care for her too as she aged. I knew from overhearing her garden conversations with my mother, that she feared euthanasia.

By summer's end after picking and shelling thousands of peas, I had become less than enthused about these in-depth explanations. Still, I listened politely as she revealed each plant's secret, unveiling the mystery of delicate tomato plants that yielded lush fruit under her care. Bent at the waist, soft ornery curls dangling before almond-shaped hazel eyes, she gently pushed away offending weeds, saying quietly, "You have to care about the details. And Paula, you will have to learn to be patient if you want to see flowers and gardens bloom." I studied the petals and, in my youthful innocence, tried to memorize each one for her sake.

I relished our time together, lingering over coffee and planning the evening's menu. Knowing I was in the presence of a profound woman, I cherished every minute. That affection is what jolted me out of bed early one summer morning when I heard the rifle blast.

Not once, but twice. Heart pounding, sensing danger, I threw on my housecoat, bounding hysterically down the circular staircase, I prayed I would not be too late to rescue her. Scary scenarios raced through my mind; memories of escaped-convict newspaper reports stole my breath.

I looked frantically out the window – only to see my grandmother in her tattered nightgown, hunting jacket thrown on top and rubber boots below (the "ear markings of a good Ukrainian"), rifle pointing to the ground, blocking my vision. She turned toward me triumphantly, rifle hoisted high in a victory dance. She had prevailed against evil.

As my heartbeat slowed, I stepped outside to see what it was she had conquered. There, its tiny legs and arms outstretched in death spasms, lay the ringleader squirrel. She had hit her mark - the bullet had found its way right between the eyes.

Stunned by the fall of her reign as my heroine, I looked to Grandpa for consolation. Realizing I had never seen Grandma put one-inch groupings in her enemies before, he called from the table where he nonchalantly chewed on toast, "Emilia! Put a pail over the squirrel."

I waited earnestly for him to right the situation, anticipating the wise words I was so accustomed to. I secretly hoped he would motion me closer to wrap me in a comforting hug.

"Well . . .," he growled instead, "those overfed squirrels should know better than to touch Grandma's pink roses."

Trained to obey, Putin stood still but he looked at me with sympathy as I squeezed shut my eyes to hold back the brimming tears. Putin had spent many summers by my grandmother's side as she solved each dilemma that arose on her land. Grandma did not believe in warning shots. It was then I realized that not all cherished life lessons arise from tender moments; some simply come from fear.

## The Sickness

As my grandparents aged, I continuously wrote them letters. Away at college, the phone was also an affordable way to hear recent news of the prairies. Grandma filled me in on details of visits when my mother had nearby business meetings. She praised neighbors who watched her precious gardens while she attended the city doctor. She complained about piles of laundry and cousins who left towels on the bathroom floor. At the sound of that dear voice, the pain of separation dissipated. I would contentedly recradle the phone, musing over her stories.

Grandma's impending kidney failure forced my grandparents to make the decision so many rural people eventually make. They purchased a home they could manage in the city, with hospital and dialysis unit nearby. They strove to enjoy their new lives as fighters, but the lack of land for a garden became heartbreaking. Away from the rural prairies they called home, winter winds became unbearable.

Throughout spring break visits, I tried to convince myself Grandma looked healthy, despite her room in the auxiliary. During our Scrabble games, I reminded her I would return each semester – assuring her I would always be back – even as she whispered, "I need you now." I did not want to see that she was deteriorating due to homesickness.

Back in my Saskatoon basement suite, I stared out dilapidated windows, desperately begging God to remind me how to breathe. It was unbearable that Grandma was forced to endure such heartache and pain after a lifetime of dedication to so many.

Too soon, I was singing *Blessed Assurance* at her funeral.

Saying goodbye to my security and my dear friend was frightening. There is a surreal calm in rural life that is lost in the metro where career opportunities are. I strove to adapt to my new surroundings and the realization that I would now have to be my own anchor. I was lost.

## Isolation

The isolated reservation where my mother worked north of Saskatoon could only be reached by airplane. Trips in and out were costly. Few professionals relish the thought of limited access to civilization and summers only with their families. I was leery of visiting my mother at the reservation – what most people call a "reserve" – because I had heard from other nurses that Northern Saskatchewan reserves are "dark" places. I misunderstood the word to mean "evil."

Although she was supportive while I was attending college, phone calls could not replace the comfort of a mother's hug. I became too focused on my neighbors shouting at midnight, frustrated at sleep interrupted by transport trucks rumbling down the freeway. Saskatoon is adventurous for the health-conscious who love riverside strolls, but not for the introverts who miss home.

I wanted to retreat, but couldn't. There was no longer a home in a cozy farming community to which I could return. Instead, I had to adjust to my new life, learning to survive like the trendy city girls who knew where the most popular restaurants were on a Friday night.

So, I shopped for black dress slacks and high heels that made sense only in the city. I learned to enjoy the symphony and cafés where neighbors recognized each other and said hello. I learned to wear earplugs to bed. As I looked out of the rustic basement apartment window sipping my espresso, I longed for my days of squirrel duty.

The dust built up in layers as the community anxiously awaited spring's return when the sun would shine regularly. A musty odor permeated the air. Unspectacular but cozy, I had decorated my entire apartment in pink – the pink of Grandma's roses. I strove for a Victorian theme, introducing accents from Paris and watercolors from Montreal.

Wanting my apartment to look elegant and cultured, I scattered books throughout the living room, never revealing even to my dearest college friends that the books simply hid carpet stains. Perhaps this is why I was touched when a neighborhood acquaintance reached out to me, inviting me to her apartment for lunch. Her acceptance, and simplicity, was a reprieve for my own expectations.

Alphonsine knew too well the grief that consumed me. The Her dear husband had died of cancer. This man, who had loved her for all that she was, left her in a high-rise apartment overlooking the river. Originally from a small town, like my grandmother she had been raised in a large farming family. Her features bespoke a First Nations heritage. Her mannerisms reminded me of the Aboriginal people I had met on the northern reserves. Quiet, she rarely revealed her grief. The pain of being alone in the city has a way of sticking to one's heart like a drizzle of glue. I knew instinctively that I should support her.

Because I had spent many holidays with my mother on northern reserves, I was somewhat familiar with First Nations people. Although the nurses' residence was fenced in to keep intruders away, I had met many of the locals while walking to the reserve's single store. The government had carved out this piece of land for the Aboriginals. Until the sixties, they could not even trade products for money off reserve. They had no vote and could not tap into modern economic markets. The First Nations people lived on this sanctioned area that resembled the shantytowns of South Africa I had seen as a child in my beloved National Geographic magazines.

Allie's round face resembled many Cree Indians I had met. Her features seemed softer others though, her smile more revealing. I welcomed having lunch with her. She often cooked homemade chicken soup, much like my grandmother had done to stay stave off winter's chill. My grandmother was called *Baba*, because we were of Ukrainian descent. Allie was referred to as a *Kookum*, the Cree word for grandmother because she was Métis Indian, which, she explained, is a blend of Canadian Indian and French or European descent. Her mother had been raised in Catholic residential schools, and then she married a French farmer. Aboriginal children had been taken from their parents on the reserve, and forced to live in dormitories run by nuns they had not previously met.

Like so many, Allie's mother was beaten for speaking Cree at the school, and subsequently did not teach her children her native language. She had raised Allie to be French like her father, yet her Aboriginal mannerisms were apparent.

Allie's heart was a servant's heart, full of her mother's love and loyalty. She was the kind of woman who daily braved snowstorms to be with her ailing grandchild in the hospital. She fervently prayed that the child would not be forgotten just because she had been born with health problems. Like my grandmother, Allie deeply feared mercy killing; she believed in the sanctity of life, standing strongly for the sanctity of human life for all ages. Like many other Canadians, Allie believed that human life was equal regardless of nationality or income.

Traditionally, First Nations people are very community focused. They do not quickly say hello, then leave. They wait with their loved ones, compassionately staying all night at a hospital bedside. They are a unit, a people who understands the strength and security in numbers. They forge a community wherever they live. Their unity encourages one another to laugh over calamity, hands over giggling mouths.

Sharing is natural for Aboriginal people, and like her people, Allie never took sides in an argument. She veiled her eyes when I complained, passively avoiding my unresolved anger. She wanted me to find peace and reconciliation.

Allie was no ordinary woman. Often alarmingly determined, she quickly spotted the political agendas of those who had them. Really, I never knew Alphonsine.

I merely encountered her like a soft cheek does the wind. Yet she became my rock in a city where I was alone without family, surrounded by fellow students who would never remember me.

I enjoyed her from a distance as I had the little native girl at my elementary school. To avoid conflict, I did not want to become too involved. I selfishly sought a neutral relationship, even though the concept was selfish - based on one person defining the relationship for the sake of comfort. I wanted to spend quality time without sharing our true beliefs – a polite Canadian relationship.

After being raised in a nation where polite indifference is applauded, Allie did not expect my loyalty. She simply hoped I would visit her in the hospital if she were sick, and protect her when she was old – like a friend should.

We became closer as we baked biscuits in her kitchen. After political studies class, I would drop in unannounced, eager to share my latest research. She looked forward to my company, and I enjoyed her rebuttals to my policy ideas. When I arrived at her boxy gray apartment, I would often reposition items on her hutch – to make it look more sophisticated. The objects seemed randomly placed. Her pictures and mismatched candles were of sentimental value. There was little color in her apartment except for the tattered orange and brown couch she would not part with. She and her husband had re-covered the furniture together. Each relic kept his memory alive.

Existing on disability income, Allie had little money to buy fashionable furniture. Still, she was satisfied with her home that welcomed strangers.

Although I was not raised to be racist, it often bothered me to share soup with her friends who dressed like social assistance outcasts. After living on the reserve and seeing children who rarely washed their hands, I obviously questioned their cleanliness too. Their smiles revealed yellow mouths stained by neglect. To Allie, however, we were all important. Neither our skin colour nor our cultural background would determine whether we were hugged. Her arms always reached out to broken angels.

As I rearranged her furniture, she asked me to help in the kitchen. Sensing my agitation around the others, she handed me a sturdy yellow bowl. Somehow rolling dough, stirring soup, and setting the table would wash fears away like washing away the dirt from her dishes. She often asked me to scoop flour out of the bag as she pounded dough on the counter. She reminded me how spoiled I was with all of my modern conveniences. On the farm, her siblings had waited all afternoon for bannock, a First Nations specialty that resembled one big square biscuit on a pan. In the northern bush, sometimes bannock would be cooked over the campfire in an iron skillet dotted with lard.

I always thought she wanted help cooking because she was disorganized in the kitchen. Not until my early thirties did I realize she was keeping me in touch with my own roots. Because Allie was Métis, her roots dangled between two cultures and she held them firmly in place. I often thought in the city, we had a wonderful opportunity to forget the past. Cities are anonymous, where everyone busily rushes to get their morning coffee then rushes home in the late afternoon to eat in front of the television. Roots, I often thought, were not for callous city dwellers; culture and loyalty were lost on them. Roots were for rural dwellers who understood the importance of choosing the burial spot, almost like the body was then putting down "forever" roots in that spot.

Allie's diabetes made her increasingly concerned about her own mortality. I also worried that she might slip through the cracks of the health care system because she was an elderly First Nations' woman with a disease common to her people.

When she told me in confidence about her blackening toe, my heart skipped a beat. I strove to remain positive even though she could sense my concern.

The doctors wanted to instantly remove the toe before the rot spread to her leg. She was not willing to make such a rash decision. A thinker by nature, she wrestled with the lonely idea of losing a part of herself, all the while her doctors accused her of negligence.

I hoped social workers would improve her living situation to accommodate her disease, but they had few answers. Instead, she was offered a room at the auxiliary wing, where she would remain a patient. She was facing the loss of a limb, not her mind, not her heart. She had fully understood the consequence of admitting to a doctor that her toe was black; she knew it was the beginning of death. She knew if she left the hospital missing one toe, she would soon lose another.

She knew as her limbs were taken, one at a time, her carcass would be hidden in a back room in a home for aging seniors – even though she was only in her late fifties. The operations would be a quick and painless process for those seeking to comply with health district policy.

Frantically, I searched for answers, unwillingly to see

her suffer as my grandmother had. Often frustrated with Allie's culture, I wanted her to engage, not passively endure the consequences of possible euthanasia. I wanted her to shed the Aboriginal skin that encouraged her to avoid resistance. To me, an invisible apartheid seemed to exist in our province, the separation of two races left unchallenged.

As I entered the hospital room and saw her lying there without a leg, I took an involuntary step backward. She lay alone, eyes shut, trying to ignore the phantom pain from her missing leg. As she endured this excruciating pain day after day without family support, I could see her pain was not phantom pain.

At her bedside I could only watch, unstoppable tears rolling down my cheeks. Allie looked like a war victim. Seeing my grief and consumed by her own, Allie quietly asked me to read her the first psalm. I drew her Bible from the drawer and read until she slept at last.

Angry, frustrated, and grieving, I believed if she would only fit into the white community I would not have to protect her, to worry about her as she aged. If she were healthy, she would be productive and deemed worthy of our free health care. Our lives would be simpler then, if she were just willing to fight the way I was. I begged her to survive. I pleaded with her to fit in so the community would value her. I wanted her to prove that she could overcome so that when she died, it would be with respect and dignity. If she did not fight, she would be prematurely buried in the country where so many other voiceless elderly lay. I did not know the true Allie.

Instead, she attended church more regularly – where people knew her name. Her rough hands lifted toward the God who loved her. With tears streaming down her weathered face, she was reminded He was her anchor. "It's not about your fight, Paula," she would say matter-of-factly.

Like me, professionals wanted to decide where her home should be – even though she already had a home. Political officials wanted to neutralize her religion, even though God had been there in her darkest moment. She would not speak, but it was her fight, not ours.

After years of personal struggle, she would never allow indifference to rob her of free will. Free will is a precious gift God gave humankind, yet is the one gift many fail to exercise properly. Through her choices, Allie reminded me that the freedom to choose a life independent of government control is the real pillar of democracy. Allie would not become a statistic about Aboriginal people and their diseases. She would not become a theory of biological warfare. Allie was alive and that will to live is was of immeasurable value.

Like my grandmother, Allie was unconcerned about social acceptance. She valued life, learning to laugh at each new issue.

Although she had lost a leg to diabetes, she offered to meet me downtown for a coffee. She also insisted on keeping her apartment, and learned to function with her new wheelchair. In a shoe store, she shocked the manager by asking if he would give her half price since she only needed one shoe. She enjoyed life and was a fighter who could take care of herself, even in her old age. She had been raised on a farm where she learned that life was precious, survival an obligation. True to herself, Allie knew pretending to be someone is hollow, even if successful. She would triumph by embracing who she was.

One Sunday afternoon, I watched her scoot about

in her wheelchair, discouraged after she lost the second leg to diabetes. At last, I began to realize she did not fear judgment from the white community. She did not feel as insecure as I had first believed. As she busied herself in the kitchen, I asked whether she needed any help. As a professional cook, I had to resist the urge to take over. Instead, I reached for the coffee and mugs that had been placed up high by unthinking visitors. I quietly brewed the coffee as she brought sautéed carrots and roasted chicken to the table.

I felt ashamed for thinking she needed my help more than I needed hers. It was then I finally understood that I was one of her lost angels, an angel who did not understand the complexities of the human heart. I did not have genuine mercy for human frailty. I had worried about her voice and her disability when I should have protected her heart and her beliefs. In leaving home, my own heart had become homeless. I was her lost angel.

"Allie," I mouthed.

"Yes," she replied, loving eyes piercing my soul.

"You are a very good cook, Allie . . . just like my Baba."

## Chapter Six

# Chief Elected

# We Arrive

My heart beat rapidly as our dark Suburban approached the entrance to Hell. Turning off the already desolate highway, we sloughed through mud, up a road to an Indian reserve that locals feared. A Northern Outpost nurse, my mother was guaranteed financial benefits after twelve months working with the people whom government employees "politically correctly" referred to as "Canadian Aboriginal." Excited about her new job, she loved the weather challenges of the North. Although she was sociable, she raved about the solitude. She was ecstatic that I could join her for the summer, ready to experience the Canadian wild. We bounced violently, hitting potholes with alarming speed. Assuring me that constant motion was necessary to prevent sinking, my stomach knotted as she described one storm where she sat stalled for hours hoping for rescue.

"Ouch," I groaned as my head hit the roof. I had never been north before and defiantly wore leather flats purchased during a sidewalk sale. My jeans were already permanently stained by muddy splatters as I climbed each day into the suburban. Black flies swarmed around my neck, winged monsters waiting to ravage my flesh. Spruce trees, bent from years of wind resistance, blocked the rays of light needed for warmth. I could feel dust from the wheels penetrate my nostrils with each breath. Clearing my throat gave a little reprieve – and an opportunity for a mosquito to explore my mouth. Each cough drew in the odour of wet moss. Clutching my water bottle like liquid gold, I winced as my mother pointed toward the deer grazing in the ditch.

As we neared a large cement tepee-like structure, she proudly announced it was the new nursing station. The new design was meant to welcome patients; to help counsellors and professionals become more culturally sensitive. This community building housed a home-care department that displayed posters encouraging mothers to bring babies in for immunization. As I toured the round hallways, I was introduced to one of the counsellors walking briskly towards her office. An Alberta rose with sharp thorns in amongst rural life, she startled me with her abrupt manner. It was immediately apparent she wanted to progress, but there were few opportunities for aggressive Aboriginal women. I later joked that furtherance also required nursing training.

Most of the other employees were more reserved, observing visitors without being intrusive. In fact, most people looked down; and only a few maintained eye contact. I would learn to enjoy the quiet strength and shy humour that Aboriginal women have. Revealing their wit, they pursed their lips at my stomach. My mother, a short friendly Ukrainian, barely made eye contact with my belly button.

Walking across the parking lot to the nurse's residence, Mother warned me that it was rarely dark in the evening. She assured me I would quickly adapt to sleeping through sunlight. I queried how the children could keep a schedule under those circumstances. One evening late at night, I heard them playing in the ditch;

I learned very few had a curfew. A high fence, fortifying the safety of the nurses from possible attack, surrounded the residence. The reserve was known for domestic disputes fuelled by alcohol consumption. My first few nights, I barely slept, trembling at the sound of gunshots. One night I peeked out the corner of the window, shivering with fright. There stood a tattered brown horse. He had sauntered past the gate, and was scratching his hind leg on the residence's cement wall. The wall shook with every powerful hip thrust. Avoiding eye contact with the bothersome beast, I covered my head with my quilt.

Each day, I sought a reason to escape the duplex. I was not permitted to walk on the roads without a nurse. Suitably accompanied, I pranced along, pink liquid patches dotting my legs, covering itchy mosquito bites. Longing for adventure, I stalked the rickety bridge, pretending to be a Loyalist spy. Strolling through the field, I could feel the eyes of locals watching our every step. Teens would shyly call out "Hi," interested in this stranger. Speaking awkwardly, they would try to impress me with their knowledge of English swear words. A young girl dressed in black welcomed me, offering a cigarette. Refusing, I boldly held eye contact even with young strangers. As I struggled to inhale dust without choking, my new-found friends warned me not to ever look in the eyes of a seer – I would lose my soul.

Later that day, sensing my boredom without my own friends nearby, my mother invited me to accompany her to the store. Against the wall sat an elderly man, with gentle eyes and an observant pose. Pointing towards him as we waddled through the mud, I asked my mother if he were a prophet. She gently pushed my finger down, scolding me for being rude. Afraid I had offended him, she hung her head to show repentance. Skilled with people, she adopted their cultural courtesies as her own. When she turned around, I stared at the man fearlessly.

The reserve had quickly become home for Mother, and she talked about the people lovingly. Some of her co-workers, intrigued by my blonde hair, were eager to know me. Honoured, she accepted these rare invitations to join them for deer soup. Their houses were two stories high, with wooden floors and unadorned walls. The single bathroom looked wet with steam along the roof, and reeked of mildew. Mud was unavoidable, so we walked through the house with our boots on. As we sat on garage sale wooden chairs, we held plastic bowls of deer soup in our hands. Chunks of meat and a few noodles floated in the brown broth. Afraid to taste unfamiliar meat, I toyed with my spoon. Encouraging me to try the soup, my mother asked what I thought. Swishing the deer around my mouth first, my taste buds eventually accepted the taste of suede. Smiling politely, I responded with a favourable review.

Our host was warmed by our kindness, and enjoyed our company. I found the visit awkward. I could not comprehend the host's happiness at sharing her small home with ten other people. She was frail and peckish from vitamin deficiency. Difficulties in shipping produce to the North limits the variety of vegetables. Yet her eyes sparkled as she offered her delicacy.

I preferred riding to the exciting powwows, protected from bugs and dust. When people offered a seat in their car, I quickly agreed. Once, we jolted suddenly as driver kicked the brakes to avoid impact with wild horses blocking the road. Grabbing the dashboard to protect my face from the windshield, I whimpered. The wild horses stood, unrelenting. The lead horse, hair scruffy brown from weathering the seasons, would not spook. He dominated the reserve. Dark, fierce eyes penetrated the soul as he held my gaze. I trembled as he sauntered closer. My friend whipped down the window, screaming in a loud authoritative, "Move!" Most of the horses moved to the side, but the boss remained. "If they don't listen, I will just inch the truck closer," she calmly exclaimed. *Oh hell no*, I thought, wanting desperately to slide into my stilettos and sprint back to Edmonton. I was meant for urban life, sipping specialty coffee and debating government mistakes. I was not meant for equine attacks in the Canadian wilderness. Honking her horn, we inched closer until the leader's face was close to my window. We passed so closely, I could feel his breath. As he eventually sauntered off the little bridge, he seemed to call out *Undwa.* Air hissed from my lungs. My sweet summer was turning out to be mind-altering.

Many of the nurses were skittish at being a minority, but my mother blossomed. Dark skinned visitors would permeate our apartment, wandering around to inspect her belongings. They looked perplexed by the number of bedrooms she had for just one person. When she opened the fridge, they were stunned, unfamiliar with the condiments filling her fridge door. They giggled, chattering about the freezer full of bagged vegetables and meat. After many visits, I had learned they pitied her for having no deer meat. Some encouraged her to find a man, so she would have deer meat. Some younger ones preferred fast food from the store already wrapped, but the older women were accustomed to brothers and husbands hunting for deer. My mother, not eager to use a rifle, assured them she would prefer a romantic suitor.

## Savages

My only evening company were adults who invited me to watch television in their apartment or police officers who came for the hot meal they had been promised months earlier. The police had very little socializing time on the reserve, despite their sanguine temperaments. They were kind men, with bags under their eyes from little rest. They rarely stayed on the reserve longer than two years, and made few attempts to put down roots. They remained all through the meal. *It must be stressful* I thought, *wearing vests and always looking over your shoulder*. They were gracious guests, but weathered by experience. Their sincere eyes lacked optimism. The North had transformed each idealist into a realist – a problem solver. Few professionals worked on the reserve for more than a summer, and returned home with impractical politics. In the North, the consequence for every decision was immediate.

I was confounded one evening when I heard a nurse label the locals "savages." I did not understand why she would work as an outpost nurse if that was how she felt about the Aboriginal people. "She is burned out," explained my mother the next morning during breakfast. The pay increase is lucrative for young nurses needing money to pay off mortgages and student loans, but not all those fresh graduates are prepared for the dynamics between the band and the government. I discovered in conversing with new graduates, just how ill prepared they are for the level of health care offered in the North, or for emergencies that arise in isolated communities. Not understanding the concept of burnout at age fifteen, I mouthed sympathetic words to the chain smokers complaining about overtime.

Daily volatile events, erratic routine and constant crime soon drained the life from the eyes of many. Watching the black body bags being loaded into ambulances evoked little emotion. The family of the man who committed suicide after murdering his girlfriend, quietly walked to their truck. I assumed that they were remorseful even though they staggered to the vehicle, expressionless. The reserve was home to less than a thousand people, and most of the families knew a situation would arise as quickly as a can of beer was opened. News had already reached the station through the children who watched the ambulance from the cover of the ditch. They quickly reported details to the curious.

Intrigued by my first experience with death, I studied the body bag from my window. The shape inside the hard plastic black bag looked too small to be the body of a grown man. I ducked quickly when an EMT looked my way. Overhearing a nurse venting, I later learned the inebriated man shot his head off with the rifle, after killing his victim in a drunken frenzy. The spacious bag with the lump inside lay on the stretcher until details were finalized and the EMT's whisked him away.

Soon afterward, important-appearing people flew in from Edmonton for a day of meetings, returning to the city as quickly as they came. This debriefing appeared exciting, and I incorporated the word into every essay I wrote the following fall. The station managers never saw the violence, the ambulances, or the fences keeping the "savages" and wild dogs out of the residence. They did not see the difficulty the planes had landing, or evenings of remorse over a death. They flew in for meetings, held in an office free of distractions, where they could wash their hands, and sit down at a boardroom table. They saw a Suburban racing up and down the runway cut from a field. They could not land in the field if horses were grazing. As they deplaned, they were driven to the station. Although I waited eagerly at the nursing station to meet them, I only saw them get back into the Suburbans that very day. Rarely did they spend the night or engage the locals.

I simply thought this aloofness was because the reserve was dusty during the summer and few visitors enjoyed muddying their dress pants. It was certainly not the setting for academics or tie-wearing professionals who could easily overlook that the nurses really needed a fan. To the locals, those managers in suits seemed so irrelevant. Architects assumed the North was cold, so the nurses worked in a building without air conditioning. When the discomfort was finally conveyed, "*Budget*" was the response.

Each afternoon I would wash my face and hair again, standing in front of the freezer to cool off from the scorching sun. Yet heat was the least of our worries; owning a fly swatter was like finding the pot of gold. Playing connect-the-dots with a felt marker and the pink welts on my legs, my summer became a journey to recover my humanity. I knew one day I would be back to interview the locals, but promised myself I would not wear a dark suit. I promised I would go outside the compound and enjoy the company of the First Nations people.

## Interview with a Chief

After a decade of visiting my mother on reserves, I was excited to interview a real chief. I knew what an honour this was for a woman, let alone a non-aboriginal. Although I had continued to connect with the community, my mother moved regularly to different reserves.

When I moved to the city, thick textbooks about public policy distracted my focus. I stirred the caramel sinking to the bottom of my macchiato, basking in spring sunshine. Lingering for hours with other academics, the difficulties travelling to the reserve had become faint memories. My apartment was cool, and the running water endless. My Métis neighbour kept me in touch with my past, yet rarely challenged my experiences. I lived alone with two cats, phoned my mother as often as possible, and read about chiefs in the newspaper. The reservation and the politics had progressed as I too matured. Unaware that chiefs were now elected, I assumed family members were still placed in power.

Chiefs were seen only from afar during my youthful visits, and their roles had changed. Now I had an opportunity to interview a chief. Even though I was briefly introduced through connections, the opportunity as an adult to converse as an intellectual was limited. My understanding of their function was coloured by my education. Growing up behind a high fence biased my experience. My experiences with the First Nations people were encounters, each leaving me with facts or emotion. My understanding of politics was based from college textbooks or the results of decisions made for the people, not by the people. I was unaware that the election process on the reserve was as democratic as in any city, and the position of chief was held for six years.

The chief's modern role as a public figure heightened their awareness of public relations, and with the aid of the media, they soon became more visible. Each reserve had council members who helped the chief decide how to allocate money, and elders who encouraged the younger generation to succeed. Wisdom and history now passed to the children through storytelling.

Chiefs were in charge, decisions final at their desks. All equally influential, they protected and empowered their people. A meeting with a chief was humbling, and my heart raced as I feared the unknown. Unsure of protocol, I decided simply to be attentive. Asking few questions and waiting for responses seemed appropriate. While attending university, I had heard negative statements from some Aboriginal students. Very few had met a chief personally. They based their opinions on gossip overheard at the bar. Few talked to a chief as a professional, and their background knowledge was minimal. Only vague memories of reserve life relieved my nervousness, memories of remarks heard at the store, or descriptions by staff at the nursing station. I had envisioned a chief to be an aging man who smokes.

I remembered hearing snide comments about chiefs' and elders' lack of education. Their ability to relate to the younger generation and their understanding of politics were questioned. They said the difficulties facing elders were too substantial to tackle. However, a local police officer reminded me that police were not hired for "social policing," implying that crime prevention ultimately rests on the shoulders of the chief. Chiefs were held responsible for the disenchantment of the youth, and obligated to channel youthful zeal into productive endeavours. As each rumour of unnecessary meetings in Las Vegas reached me, they left my conscience wanting. Determined to seek guidance, I accepted an opportunity to speak with a chief, free of assumptions and my own agenda. The opportunity was an entrance into a locked world. Because of my respect for First Nations people, I would remember and cherish every detail. Each concept revealed, if properly phrased questions were asked, would reveal the dynamics of modern leadership.

When I met the chief and his wife, they were very respectful. He was younger than I had envisioned, and not at all like movie stereotypes. Stocky, poised, and humble, his eyes radiated strength and vision. Unintimidated by the pending interview, he invited me to take a seat. The colourful restaurant appealed to young adults, the smell of buffalo chicken wings wafted by our table.

Scanning the menu, I reminded the chief and his wife that I promised to pay for dinner, to thank them for taking time from their very busy schedules. Watching his face as he spoke to the waitress, the chief reminded me of a strong professor, well read and always curious. Undisturbed by my gawking, he patiently waited as I frantically flipped through my journal pages.

I learned he and his wife had attended university, and had a background understanding of the challenges students face while attending college in the city. Through the complexities of urban culture, young people gain the wisdom for survival in both cultures.

Poised, the chief was unwilling to engage in an argument. Instead, he engaged me in political conversation as soon as the waitress returned with our coffee.

Anticipation had distracted me from enjoying my breakfast. Now I wanted fruit, which would be neat to eat. Finger foods are an appropriate food choice when trying to hide neurotic authorial tendencies and caffeine-induced tension. Unfortunately, I settled on nachos.

It became increasingly difficult to impress the chief with my interview skills as cheese, tomatoes, and every ingredient that my professors and counsellors had warned me against oozed off the nachos. It proved difficult to get the cheese safely into my mouth while asking about loans given as vote-earning tactics. My fleece jacket and slacks itched to be spilled on. The distractions lessened my ability to confront the politics effectively.

Motioning the waitress respectfully, he asked her to bring cream for the coffee. She complied with reverence. She had obviously met him before and respected him.

This chief smiled at my nervous behaviour, inquiring about my book. Flattered, I explained my research regarding provincial spending. Originally, the research was intended as a graduate school proposal. Eventually it evolved into a controversial journal. He nodded with genuine interest, responding with details about the current plans for oil and mining in the province. Not only was Alberta active, but my home province of Saskatchewan was booming with industry. Unfortunately, in Saskatoon, housing availability had not caught up with need. Many Aboriginal people were desperate for housing. It seemed as oil was discovered, housing and wages disappeared. I told him about urban ghettos in my town, and how houses were becoming unaffordable for those on social assistance or disability. I complained how there would soon be little refuge left for the homeless – often First Nations people – and my fear that my diabetic friend would slip through the cracks of economic change.

As we talked, his educational background and love of science became apparent. He was well read and up-to-date with the latest medical approaches for diabetes. Knowing my concern, he assured me that there was a progressive approach to combating diabetes in the United States and it would be only a matter of time before Canada developed a cure.

"Funding for diabetes?" I asked.

Ignoring my sarcasm, he detailed with optimism how cures for diabetes were possible. Believing that change required action, he assured me that cures were being fought for. Even accountability for loans – instead of using them for political popularity – was achievable. Awkwardly I looked away, forgetting I had mentioned the dilemma earlier. He explained how change evokes an array of different opinions. It requires new actions with new convictions. Change is time sensitive, yet worth fighting for. Each word caught my genuine interest, and was given purposefully. The chief did not demand respect; he commanded respect.

I felt sheepish, revealing that I had only brought with me a journal and a pen. He was not arrogant, nor did he have that academic ego that some graduates carry with them. He had been a student and a teacher. He had been a warrior and a peacemaker. Each scar, visual and non-visual, reminded me of his battles. His scars were earned in a battle he was not willing to share with this unprepared young woman. His eyes told me he had been left with a challenge. Political accountability requires the consent of the people who voted for him. It was not an unattainable dream if the people themselves believed. Unfortunately, very few change along with politicians if their lifestyle is challenged. A chief who inherits debt, along with the demands of modern accountability, needs great bargaining skills and wisdom. I could only imagine the stress of leading people while promoting change. His sharp mind and piercing eyes betrayed a gentle spirit. It became clear to me: his role in society was deeply misunderstood.

It was obvious he wanted to embrace a history of culture and tradition, yet fifty percent of reserve youth migrate to the city. Without young people to marry and produce, a community becomes populated with the aged. A region without youth is also a region that is not economically advancing.

Although the chief maintained the privacy saved for leadership, he knew that my generation was calling for answers about financial waste. They had seen employees with modest positions driving expensive Cadillacs. They had seen band members going to Las Vegas while ordinary people lost their houses to black mould. Rumours said chiefs were seduced into spending reserve royalties, yet he had arrived in a practical four-door car like his other employees drove.

To be clear, I asked him to explain just the basics of his role. Even with a public administration degree, it was obvious I knew little.

"What is the role of a chief?" I asked hesitantly, not only curious about the response, but also hopeful it would spark a story.

He looked down, pensive, a man who did not want to misuse words. Traditionally, First Nations men like to mean what they say. They are not quick to respond, and would rather remain silent than speak out of turn. Wanting me to understand, he began explaining his background role. Historical understanding is necessary in order to envision the future role of chief, he said. Without knowing the history of First Nations people, it would be simplistic to offer advice for their future. Intellectuals have become knowledgeable of statistics, yet ignorant of basic personal experience. First Nations agendas have become trendy. As he spoke, I continued to munch my messy nachos, just as I had in my childhood when my father told me a story. My eyes glittered with anticipation as he stroked his chin. The moment itself was delicious; the story would linger in my mind for years.

"A long time ago," he said methodically, "the chief's role was functional."

He paused, careful to expand the thought in the right direction. He was not distracted by the noise of the restaurant or the waitress who interrupted with more coffee.

"In the winter, the people needed to be taken care of," he said. "They gathered together in groups for survival. Often the groups were a couple of families. A man took the lead role naturally and was respected by the people. The families would trust him, because he made sure that they had food in winter and the families would have enough shelter and protection."

I was intrigued by his choice of words and his choice to omit tribal names. I recalled watching movies where young men vied for power. The struggle for power occurs throughout history regardless of national background. Not so, he explained, for First Nations people, the chief's role is functional.

"In the nomadic days, the weather, and the raw need for survival would draw families to cluster in winter for protection. The family unit is very important for First Nations people, and the chief was a man who ensured their safety and collective protection from the elements and themselves. The families would then spend the summers independently, near the lakes, enjoying their family and working together during the warmth of the summer sun," he said. "Have you read the book 1491?"

"Uh, no, I have not," I said, trying to change the subject to appear well read. I had decided the minute I ordered my nachos to disguise my ignorance and my lack of academic reference. I was a people person, much more intrigued by autobiographies and an occasional women's exercise magazine that could show me how to develop six pack abs in thirty days. I learned over the years that those abs are hidden under piles of college-day nachos. Unfortunately, I had learned Aboriginal culture by osmosis. Encountering First Nations people expanded my once limited views, but did not give me a balanced view.

"1491 was a book that explained the life as it was before the Europeans arrived with their desire for land, and their biological warfare. These lakes used to be filled with tents over the summer by our people who loved to camp and enjoyed the land. The biological warfare wiped out our race, our people."

As he talked, I realized he was alluding to First Nations people who were not immune to new European diseases, those victimized by the sicknesses settlers and traders brought. Seeing that I was perplexed, he reminded me how European diseases had a much greater debilitating force than their negotiating skills. He reminded me how the stench of buffalo carcasses and human bodies tainted the air. The nomads were self-indulgent aristocrats. *Perhaps fast food chains were modern warfare*, I mused, but remaining quiet seemed wisest.

"So the people camped around the lakes in the summer?" I asked.

He nodded. As a teenager, I had learned to watch faces, because most Aboriginal people motion direction and moods with their mouths. On the reserve, many speak mainly with eye and lip movement. Driving a kookum home once, we got lost for thirty minutes because I missed which way her lips pointed. People of British descent are often expressionless when they speak, making the voice inflection hard to follow. Not all Aboriginal people who leave the reserve are proficient in English. Perhaps that is why they become so frustrated with the white culture when they move to the city. Yet the fact that they can handle two languages speaks volumes about their learning potential.

"They have no choice," he continued with regret, not unlike a father seeing his children suffer.

"Young people must venture out now, find work, and some self respect. They must go, regardless of the past. You see the alcoholism? The destitution? That stems from the lack of employment and opportunities for our youth. They must venture out and experience life. They must be able to work and feel the satisfaction and reward of providing for their family. Realistically the band, and other organizations on the reserve, can only hire less than 15 percent of the community. The younger generation needs to be involved with progressive thought," he said passionately.

I knew some felt the sting of racism, others culture shock. I thought about my best friend in high school who is Métis. Although she struggled to stay clean from her past drug addiction, the city seemed to swallow her up like rain down the gutter. She tried to overcome stereotypes, social assistance, and a broken past, but each attempt failed. She returned to those human traffickers. Her own people did not uphold her dream. They did not protect the family she loved or the wonderfully decorated house in the town she called home. She was only looking for a home, for better opportunity. Instead, she ended up looking in the mail for government cheques, eventually living homeless.

The memories intruded, interrupting my concentration. I could not erase flashbacks of her situation. I dreaded knowing her fate – was she a prostitute once more?

I told the chief how the media had labelled Saskatoon "Harlem of the Prairies." I explained how many previous residents hated First Nations people because of robberies propagated by gang members. Urban reserve is what the media has called these unfortunate neighbourhoods. Gangs seem to pack together for a sense of tribe, longing for a family.

The chief was well aware of the statistics and overwhelming realities First Nations leaders face. Like a father, he assured me that my generation needs to be brave in the light of change. We need to be innovative in the times of chaos. We need to be passionate about learning in the midst of hopelessness. When a generation feels hopeless, they stop hearing, he said. They ignore learning and disdain change. Without learning, a generation cannot grow, and growth is necessary for a nation to produce.

In essence, he continued, without hope, our economy dwindles. Without hope, we remain unhealed. Years of history have repeated themselves because Canadians felt that helping Aboriginal people is hopeless. Aboriginal youth have stopped dreaming because they see the lack of opportunity, and give up hoping that one day things will be better. Once again, the Canadian people continue living disinterestedly, repeating what their fathers did, because talking truthfully would be hopeless.

"Look at the Chinese people," he said shrugging. "They endure racism, yet they work hard and carry on with their pursuits. These people have an inner fortitude that we, as a culture, need. We have to decide to work hard and succeed in spite of dismal circumstances." His shoulders slumped, disheartened, as he spoke of other cultures who endured racism yet contributed to society. He was genuine in his resolve to see a young generation go out and succeed, knowing they could always come home to their tribe when they had succeeded. There would be land for them to retire on, once they were older. Like their forefathers, they would sit by the lake after a winter of surviving. The lake was a reward for the year's hard work.

Although the chief at first seemed to be an optimist, it was evident that he was, in fact, a realist. Advancing as a race is going to take an inner resolve to go beyond racism, he said. To remain undefeated in spirit would require a powerful force and resolve. That resolve was in his eyes, even though his reservation was not there yet.

His function would go beyond the simple expectations of fiscal decision-making. Modern leaders want more than votes; they need credibility. They want lasting change which takes hard work.

The ability to embrace the future without hesitation requires hope. Without land, they were homeless. Without a dream of the summer months, they were hopeless. His role now was to protect his people during the winter months, so that each family could enjoy summers by the lake. Like the chiefs of old, his function was to guide their survival through the long winter months, allowing them the independence during the summer to be a family.

Our conversation reminded me of a political rally I once attended. Our soon-to-be provincial premier chanted, "Hope beats fear." Mesmerized by his eyes, I missed details of his speech even though it radiated from his heart. His words were accurate, and his advice relevant – unlike those people who flew to reserves in black suits. Perhaps if we dared to hope, we could defeat the past that haunts us. With hope, we can resolve the mess our forefathers left behind.

We expect accountability from the First Nations people, yet minimize our own accountability. Perhaps if the younger generation dares to hope again, we could conquer our fear of the new global economy, and forge new relationships that we have been hesitant to build.

*Hope could beat fear,* I began to think, as I looked into the chief's eyes. I could see how the leadership amongst Aboriginal and non-Aboriginal were all being challenged to remain credible, to be accountable. If both cultures continue the cycle of hopelessness, history will once again repeat itself. Treaties will remain unresolved, needless death will air on the evening news, racism will continue to rob the future.

"I think perhaps," I admitted shyly, "that I am one of many who does not understand the role of chief."

I began imagining my own summers filled with warmth, a breeze blowing off the lake. Families camping, laughing together over a simple meal cooked over a large campfire. I began to believe it is possible for Canadian people to linger by still cool waters, to watch the waves wax and wane. I began to imagine a summer relieving the stresses of a winter endured and a battle won, a land of living skies we could all come home to.

Although I was skeptical, I was desperate to believe the chief, to believe him because my generation needs hope. I was desperate to believe him because it is critical for my generation to know that we can all come home again.

## Chapter Seven

# FLOJA

# Betrayal

My eyes blurred, and struggled to refocus. The sting of oil wafting from the kitchen briefly mesmerized me. Laughter boomed around the corner as I strained to hear the Latino music. My friend and I were waiting to be seated in a trendy El Salvadoran restaurant new to the city, a great contrast to my favourite neighbourhood dwelling. The press had nicknamed the area "the Harlem of the Prairies," where few businesses survived. Down the street stood dilapidated houses and apartments with barred windows. Wire fences enclosed parks littered with garbage and the used needles of drug addicts. The lively Spanish establishment dwelt in the heart of the misfortunate and the misunderstood. It brought new life to the gray, dusty end of town where it was common to see drunken men and women shouting at one another in an angry stupor even during the day.

The streets wore danger like a mantle, graffiti marking gang territory on walls, trains, and garbage bins. Tennis shoes hung from wires, reminding visitors to be careful, especially if they arrived sporting the colours of rival gangs. Businesses were routinely burglarized; cautious locals parked their vehicles within eyeshot while eating lunch.

Yet the seduction of authentic El Salvadoran fare dissolved caution. The exotic restaurant was in the heart of the aboriginal community, named by locals the "Urban Reserve." The west side was considered a wasteland where disgruntled First Nations people came to flee the reservation. Some were recruited by gang leaders, and accepted their one-minute beating to earn their colours. The city was a way to escape a small community that seemingly offered very little for the youth.

I dreaded parking my car in this neighbourhood notorious for violent crime. During my visit, an Aboriginal man staggered down Twenty-second Street screaming, "You @#$% whore" at his common-law wife; the inebriated woman promptly returned his drunken vitriol. Garbage lay on the roads, and gang members strutted like politically endorsed landowners; yet locals dared come to the lively Latin establishment, drawn by the ordinary food and promise of a refuge from the cold prairie winter. Lemon Tortilla soup could drain a sinus infection better than any doctor's prescription.

Most of the servers were Spanish women with long, flowing, black hair, radiant smiles, and a smouldering walk as they brought smoothies churned out of fresh fruit. Authentic Chille Rellenos were not recklessly baked on grills the way the take-out places did. They were prepared fresh, with a perfection only Maria could produce. From El Salvador, Maria's youthful smile contrasted with her aging eyes. She slapped *papusas* into perfect circles, shaking her head with disappointment to shame lax kitchen helpers.

At the back of the restaurant were paintings of beautiful Mexican women. The artist understood the difficulty of these women's daily tasks in searing summer heat. Each depicted a harmonious combination of

Old World and modern thought, but the stories on the wall faded into the background as customers became entranced by huge television screens broadcasting lively soccer matches. The sport took precedence in Europe, where passionate fans would walk for hours to watch a single game. The Latin people hiked in the searing heat just to play. Groans of the locals announced when players missed the net.

The owner was sociable and cared about his customers, each welcome amongst the Latin community. Sauntering to the tables, he chanted "Hola," while regulars shared their latest news. Most of the community respected this father figure who embraced the challenge of change. Kindly greeting customers and people in the community, he listened earnestly as they bemoaned the snow. Nodding in sympathy, he would suggest a good book to distract them. Learning warmed the soul, he said, and anchored the mind during the winter storms.

I even attempted a little Spanish, trying to prove I was multicultural. The owner winced forgivingly, asking me to repeat after him as he pronounced the words properly.

As I sat with my friend, I noticed a new server standing by the bar. This frail, waiflike girl had eyes similar to Giselle's. Catching me off guard, I stared rudely. Her smile was awkward, yet we laughed at every witty barb she uttered. Although her eyes drooped, her laughter made her intriguing. Clutching her mouth to conceal her teeth, I knew she was Aboriginal. Dressed in black, with high heels that made my shoulders tense in sympathy, she sheepishly brought water, excusing her inexperience. My friend, noticing her shoes, asked how long she had been waitressing.

"This is my first day," she sighed, "my name is Corilene."

As she spoke, her stomach caved and ribs protruded.

"It looks like I will be here all day," she moaned.

"All day in those shoes?" we gasped.

"I will be fine," she assured us. "I like working; it keeps me busy."

In this neighbourhood, it was wise not to allow a story to go any further, uninvited. Aboriginal people are often introverted, offended by too many questions. Corilene's shoulders hunched over her slight frame, yet her laughter seemed to expand her chest. She was a dichotomy of everything I learned in Native Study classes. She was her own person, yet desperately seeking compassion and approval from those around her.

Ducking her head to the right, Corilene would lean until complimented. In need of constant reassurance, she would look away, body posed submissively. I knew if I pushed hard enough she would cry, yet wipe the tears and never leave. My university education had taught me that Aboriginal people retreat, yet with every question Corilene revealed more. Textbooks taught that First Nations people are soft spoken, yet Corilene's voice carried like the El Salvadoran's. She was tougher than my former high school friend, and the 11 hours she worked that day proved it. Corilene was quick to refill water glasses, standing nearby with a water jug and a servant's smile.

"Working here is better than being alone in my apartment," she admitted. "Oh! I forgot!" as she sped away.

Gazelle-like in her awkward beauty, Corilene

fetched my strawberry smoothie. I noticed even when men suggested she was beautiful, until convinced, she would cover her mouth with a hand. Despite her intelligence, the bartender addressed her with contempt, repeatedly explaining her job description in broken English. As she walked away, he muttered in Spanish. I was so impressed at the long day she put in while wearing those impossible shoes that I easily overlooked the faults her co-worker attacked. I was intrigued whether she would last, knowing the owner often hired Aboriginal people but not many attended work consistently. Looking around for one of his latest hire, he would shrug, signifying she had not returned. The daily grind of serving food is unattractive.

The Spanish are notorious for being industrious, intolerant of a lackadaisical work ethic. Passionate and intense, they cooked food with perfection. Workers were willing to train employees who were willing to learn – so long as they kept pace. Hardworking immigrants were a contrast to those who claimed dependence on government assistance.

Savoury sauce-dripped enchiladas rewarded our lengthy wait. I yearned to watch this waitress who soon consumed my thoughts like an addiction. I found her unique personality refreshing, a diversion in my busy city life. She was unassuming and gracious. Capable of enlivening an ordinary day, the simple tasks she executed seemed delightful. She tried hard to make people happy, even though her own joy was missing.

While cooking at the hospital cafeteria one day, I looked up, and was shocked to see Corilene. Staring blankly at the food, she listlessly chose the casserole. Unable to shake her distraction, she muttered to herself, unaware of strangers watching.

"Hey you!" I called cheerfully. "You going to have any of my food today?"

She attempted to smile, failed, and explained that her aunt, who had been a mother to her, was upstairs facing death. I empathized. Losing my own aunt to cancer, I understood Corilene's grief.

Corilene explained that her own mother, who had promised never to leave, had gone on before. Now her aunt, who had become close friend and counsellor, was also losing her own life. Corilene felt abandoned. We briefly shared our heartbreak while I put food on a plate; she would not eat it. Most Aboriginal people are family-oriented and close-knit; death has a huge impact. Yet, Corilene reminded me quietly, sometimes families are not quick to forgive.

Her head hung low, and her sister seemed to be mourning at a funeral. It is a shame, I thought, that the only time hospital staff gets to see Aboriginal people is when they are sick and frail. Out in the bush, many of the elderly are energetic and resourceful. When young men help kookums like Allie pick berries, at the roar of a bear, they run for refuge in the truck cab faster than the most powerful athlete. Yet when they are losing a mother at the hospital, they are helpless. A son is broken by the sight of his mother, lying peacefully in death, swaddled in white. Their time to mourn is sacred and very personal.

The next day at the restaurant I asked Corilene if she was all right; she simply looked down. Natives often avoid conflict and feelings they are not willing to address by ending eye contact. I remembered that they also have their own sense of timing.

*How do we know when the elders are finished their 'time of mourning?'* I wondered. If an elder is interrupted before she finishes, her message will never be heard. As an impatient city girl, I could not understand this concept of time. Apparently it was simple: when they were ready, they were ready. When they grieved, they grieved until they were finished. Since meeting Corilene, I have learned the process will be as long as it takes, and until then she will avert her face to avoid questions. Instead of speaking about her aunt or mother, she smiled as she described her daughter.

I was immediately shocked to discover Corilene had a daughter. She looked too young to have a child. Apparently Angel was a lively and feisty little girl, just like her mother, and the child lived on the reservation with her grandfather. Although Angel proclaimed she wanted to live in the city, she was kept on the reserve at her grandmother's request. Until her grandmother passed away, her life was to be protected. Preserving Corilene, she helped in every way a caring mother could, rubbing her daughter's swollen legs and aching back. Yet Corilene doubted her own success as a mother, watching her mother's giving nature. Corilene questioned if she could love as deeply as her mother.

Interrupting, I suggested perhaps she should consider going back to school, assuming that she had little education. With some college background, she could provide a better life for her child. I was wrong about Corilene's education. She had already attempted a post secondary program; but only a month after she came to the city to better herself, her mother fell ill and died.

Knowing that we were both busy with work and life, I invited Corilene to join me for supper. It would be a relief to eat dinner with someone who understood the industry. She admitted to me one afternoon, as I munched on the ribs left on her plate, that she was lost. I understood, and explained how I felt homeless when my grandmother died, because my anchor was gone. We briefly looked into each other's eyes with quiet understanding.

Corilene was a mother looking for a mother. Unable to cope with the shock and fear of living life alone at the time of her mother's death, she became addicted to drugs. Her mothers kindness was her only hope, during painful winters in the city. She often wrote in her journal, questioning the cruelties of reservation life. Angry that she had a daughter, she was reminded that she was incapable of providing. It was not about the failure; she was just consumed with grief. "*Drugs simply made everything better,*" she whispered.

Corilene was not prepared for what life would bring. She did not have the ability to cleanse the shame that pulsed through her frail veins when she was sober. She had emotionally abandoned the child she adored. One winter, when cars were seemingly owned only by the wealthy, Corilene and her daughter waited for a cab. Angel screamed as the cold penetrated her little hands. Corilene rushed her daughter into the house, running warm water over her frozen hands, and frantically massaging them. She opened her shirt and put her Angel's tiny fingertips against her chest to warm them. Anything – she would have done anything – to help her beloved child. Frostbitten, the skin on her daughter's little finger tips soon began to peel. Improperly prepared for winter life on the prairies at minus 40, she was a mother who needed a mother to show her the basics of raising a child.

Discouraged, overwhelmed by remorse, Corilene slowly dialled the phone.

With a shaky voice and consumed with a sense of failure, through tears she explained to her angry father that she just could not do the parent thing right. Wanting a better life for her daughter, she asked him to take Angel to live with him. Frustrated and protective of his granddaughter, in a moment of rage he accused Corilene of being a failure, useless, incapable of doing just one thing right.

"I did not want her to become me – an angry addict – one day," she said. So Angel lived in a home where she could sleep at night.

Sipping my ginger ale, I tried not to choke on tears when Corilene called herself a failure. To live free of addictions, Corilene had to make sound decisions every day. She wanted true inner joy, but everything seemed messed up. It would be better for her daughter to be with a grandfather who loved her and knew how to keep her warm. Corilene tried to convince me that life would be better alone, with her journal and her thoughts. Rehab now over, she did not want to fall into the drug trap again, but the darkness can be consuming.

I reminded her how I had lived with a best friend who daily fought the demons that come with sobriety. She nodded but said she did not want to hear the echoes of loneliness. Her daughter would be safe and she would hear her reassuring voice on the phone whenever she could afford a phone card. The only difficulty would be to disguise the discouragement and lingering pain. Like her daughter's tiny fingers, Corilene's heart had been frostbitten.

To keep busy, Corilene worked many shifts in the lively restaurant full of others avoiding similar struggles. The Latin Americans understood what it was like to face frustrating odds and a life of toil. At the end of each night, they threw themselves into dancing with the same passion they had shown for their daily work. They were survivors, and Corilene knew they could teach her to fight for her dreams. By his very fatherly nature, the owner would teach her sound work ethics. *Keep washing dishes and making wise choices,* she told herself.

Her friend Armando shadowed her like a guard dog protecting the establishment. An achiever who took pride in his workplace, Armando's strong work ethic and sarcasm unfortunately often brought the girls to tears. Corilene was an exception – her protection was the name he had dubbed her. He called her Floja, which he said meant beautiful.

After years of failure, a single kind word could touch her cracked heart. She worked hard to please Armando, as everyone did. Even customers sat up straighter when he wiped down the bar. He would not allow the restaurant to be defiled by poor work ethics. He demanded loyalty from his peers and boss alike, and he insisted that details matter, but sweet Corilene was a people person who often forgot where she had left her pen.

"Look around," he would snap in broken English, "tell me you don't see what needs doing."

He often scowled, pulling out a pile of clean dishes that needed putting away, or putting dishes back in the sink because they were not clean enough. There was no reason to be walking around like a fool, while tabletops needed clearing, he said. Armando did not hold back.

Fearless in the presence of hostility, he disdained the lazy and ignorant. His own English seemed to improve monthly because he was intense, and driven to achieve self-imposed goals. He had few friends, and although he pushed Corilene away with his sharp tongue and raspy disposition, she remained steadfastly loyal. Corilene endured Armando like the inevitable winter wind that howled with a vengeance. Yet below that exterior roughened by city life, her words were remained gentle, like a summer breeze off the lake.

Corilene worked haphazardly around the snarly bartender, just as she fumbled through life. On the fridge, Armando painted a picture with his words, helping her to overcome her inability to notice details, having patience with her Fetal Alcohol Syndrome (FAS) symptoms. I watched them argue one afternoon while waiting for my beef tacos. She would turn to me, explaining the difficulties of FAS. He would snap back, "Change your thoughts," in the middle of his accusations. She followed Armando around because she admired his work ethic and his ability to focus. When he spoke respectfully of co-workers' feelings, they all followed him loyally. He had lived the life of a vagrant, exploited for his work ethic. He wore his attitude like a gun on his hip, calling it like it is and reminding friends by his actions that he needed no one. Wholly independent, he allowed very few to touch the heart he disguised with his own addictions. Corilene needed him.

Armando had learned to trade his dress shirt for groceries in the Mexican village where he waited tables. Accustomed to impressing tourists, he earned tips by laying a smile over his frown. The self-seeker disapproved of feelings, a luxury only more prosperous nations could afford. In a fit of frustration one afternoon, Armando told me that men work hard and confidently look up as they keep moving. Only the lazy, whom he disdained, would whine when hard work has to be done. Needing people was weak, he said, and crying over loss was pathetic.

I admired Armando's work ethic and stamina, but he sacrificed relationships for the exhilaration of that momentum. His journey was for the lonely, and Corilene quickly became used to his curt responses, learning to keep pace with his demands. She complied with ten-hour days and sought out jobs that needed doing. Recognizing Armando's disdain for emotion, she would feel for them both.

Eager to impress her boss, one afternoon she revealed that Armando had nicknamed her Floja. Clearly upset, the boss asked her what it meant to her. Armando told me it means beautiful, she replied, cringing as she saw her boss flinch. He called Armando over to confront him.

"Tell her what it means," he said quietly but insistently. "Tell her what you've been calling her."

Corilene hung her head, already anticipating he had betrayed her.

"It means lazy," Armando said sheepishly, "you are lazy."

Corilene was stunned. That single word had shored her up during her first month of work – a word crafted by an enemy. How could she recover when a supposed friend had robbed her of hope? It made her feel ugly and worthless, a woman used by a man incapable of love. She now believed that she would continue to fail; to live the rest of her life in a vortex of underachievement. She would never again try to please Armando, never trust him again. She let her desire to be cared about dissipate. The boss, trying to salve hurt feelings, asked gently, "What do you want to be called, Corilene?"

"I want to be a hard worker, I want him to call me a hard worker," she said.

"Then, if you work hard and find things to do around here, we will call you *Trabalajar,*" he said.

## Trabalajar Blossoms

*Trabalajar* means "hard worker" in Spanish. Called a failure by her own father and despised by her own neighbourhood, Corilene needed a respectful name. She needed a name that redefined who she was and all she could accomplish. She needed words of kindness and encouragement, so that she could face the darkness of night. She would earn this new name with her own strength.

That small hope fueled her, lifting her spirit. She did want to be a hard worker and she wanted Armando's respect. Corilene would prove to them all that she was indeed a *trabalajar.* It was not about reputation now, it was about self respect. This was a personal victory she needed to win, a moment in life when she stepped out of the bog to embrace the city lights. This defining moment would alter her destiny. One day Angel would see their home rebuilt by her mother's determined hands.

I would bump into Corilene at lunch, then see again her in the evening. She and the cooks would tease me about my beef taco addiction. I noticed she had begun to remember details. Her clarity and sense of self were obvious. Although she remained reserved, her words became bolder, her sense of belonging more secure. I was surprised and to see that a friendship with Armando could be rewarding. As I sipped my soda, I watched Corilene multi-task with ease, pleased but feeling guilty for staring.

I enjoyed Corilene's company. She was a rare woman who understood loyalty and often put my mind at rest from the stress of too much thinking. She encouraged me to change my thoughts, grinning as she made a combo for me. Her wisdom increased as her self confidence grew. Her presence was needed at work – they were short-staffed during the dinner rush without her constant dedication. Armando and Corilene had become a team, developing an intriguing friendship. He was the leader, the strength that Corilene needed follow. She desperately wanted him to call her *Trabalajar*, she would work hard in order for him to mean it.

Joking around one day, we began to talk about Armando. I remarked how the restaurant was clean, but her eyes seemed glazed. Armando is preoccupying your mind, I suggested. No, she explained, a story she had read was inspiring her.

The story was about two brown horses struggling with their journey. One was blind and the other wore a bell to guide the blind horse. As she related the tale, my stomach lurched and my palms began to sweat. The "horse" had marked her, as he had marked me. Relating how the horses matched pace as a team, her excitement radiated.

Feigning interest, I nodded, eager to escape our conversation. I did not want Corilene to see my mistrust of the chocolate-brown horse. Yet she continued to speak with respect about him, identifying with this creature of mystery. Slowly backing out of the restaurant, I felt nervous the entire drive home.

One afternoon, I invited her out to join me for some Asian food, so neither of us would be reminded of bad childhood memories. At the table off in the corner of a Vietnamese restaurant, she told me she had oddly called out Armando's name in a moment of despair at her aunt's funeral. The immense grief consumed her, but she was proud of herself for working through the issues. Then looking away rather than down, she suggested, "I was probably wanting my father, but Armando's name was the one I called. My father wasn't looking for me, so I wasn't looking for him."

Shrugging, she looked away to prevent the embarrassment of public tears. Yet a couple drops escaped her eyes, leaving me helpless. Change is difficult. "Maybe I needed Armando to tell me that I was a *trabalajar* because I felt like I had failed my father."

Without reassurance or a healthy respect from a father, a child wanders aimlessly. An insecure woman makes the impulsive decisions of a frightened little girl. Although our conversation reminded me of my own relationship with my father, I did not feel empathy for her. I knew that her father had helped her get clean of her addictions and selflessly raised the child she now missed and loved. After his wife's death, he tried desperately to rebuild a home for his children. He had discovered that the strength of a family reveals the strength of a nation.

I understood her need to erase past mistakes, to discover that she could rebuild. She wanted to prove to her father and to Armando that her name would be unforgettable. Through her, I realized that many of us have been raised to believe respect is earned. In reality, respect is given. She was worthy of our respect even before she started working.

Building a community is more memorable than destroying one. She earned her new name "*trabalajar*" by her decisions and her actions, and soon became the favourite of many of the regulars. Corilene was a beautiful rose that had blossomed in the middle of the rugged prairies. Soon, her family would linger near the summer lake, basking in the scented breeze.

Even though she was raised as First Nations on a reservation, like any other transplanted girl in the city, she longed to return home, but a house had not yet been built. The process takes patience, time for the foundation to expand and contract. Each howling storm would be an opportunity for her to grow. Weathered by life, her words would soften with earned self-respect. Armando would finally realize that he needs someone, and Corilene would rediscover her capacity to give. Her name would be seen by the world on the internet, and one day she will finally hear those precious words, *I am looking for you.*

Chapter Eight

# GANG PUNK

# Philosopher

In prison, inmates join gangs or die. Criminals are feared social deviants, admired by youth. While paying their time, gangsters in this town are sought out by conference organizers needing a public lecturer in the North. The speaker warns young men on the reserve to avoid jail, showing them his forearm tattoo while watching his back. He is marked for life, yet I cannot publish his name. I was cautioned it could mean death.

I became desperate to find a man willing to disclose the intricacies of criminal behaviour. Each interviewee had backed down, refusing to answer my calls simply because I mentioned gangs. The concept of crime seduced me. The deeper the research, the more the information pulses through my veins like a drug. *Which gang punk gave Angel Dust to the children?* I wanted to know.

Each roadblock strengthened my belief that I should return home to speak with my father, who had retired from the police force when I was little. As a student, I had been surprised to learn that gangs do not commit the majority of violent crimes. Yet newspapers describe gangs as local terrors. I knew that my father was fearless and that he would have answers to my questions. A philosopher, he lived like a hobbit in northern Ontario. His books randomly filled the house, dusty yet challenging. Spending his evenings reading the newspaper, my father kept his mind alert, a general in the old academic guard.

The long drive to Thunder Bay is arduous for the impatient traveller. The prairies are beautiful, but after looking at the same straight road and the same golden fields, they all began to blend into one hypnotic mirage. Slapping my legs to wake up, I decided to stop in Brandon, which had a coffee shop with really good coffee. I would then spend the night in Winnipeg, with its funky restaurants and friendly locals.

A good friend living in Winnipeg had her car vandalized by gang violence, which seemed to confirm the research indicating that gangs are the biggest reason for break and enters. Statistically, gang activity only accounts for 16 percent of violent crimes committed in the nation. More than 70 percent is due to domestic violence.

News reports of recent murders raced through my head as I hit the straight stretch, ocean waves of wheat filling the fields. Daydreaming passed the time while traversing the land of living skies. I smiled, recalling trips with college friends on this very road, and how much I enjoyed hearing my Eastern friends ask, "Is this it?" I used to live for that moment, enjoying their facial expressions as they realized that no one was around to see. The East is so heavily populated with busy traffic, a true concrete jungle. Crime is rising in the East, along with its population. It seems that every inch of land in the East is taken, while in the sparsely populated prairies, the air is peaceful and the nights are lonely for a dreamer.

# Details

The morning after I arrived at my father's home, I looked out the kitchen window to see if it had snowed. Thunder Bay is the only city that has no snow throughout January and February, then a record-breaking pile falls at the end of March. The Sleeping Giant overlooking the Great Lake enjoys being mischievous, convincing the clouds to release one last dump. I knew the snow would make my father less willing to walk down the block to our favourite Scandinavian restaurant. Waiting for my coffee to heat in the microwave, I watched my father's adopted birds chirping at each other in his backyard.

Each year his birdhouses multiply. He is the only one in the neighbourhood concerned about their homelessness. In the middle of a wild winter, birds chirp with delight because my father ritualistically brings seeds out to them. I was convinced that my sister and I need not worry about global warming; the animals would be safe in our backyard.

Grumbling and loud thumping on the staircase signalled my father's approach. It was as though a life of hard work had consumed the last of his energy.

He was an ex-policeman, city-employed, author, academic, researcher, and grandpa wrapped around the finger of an energetic toddler. At university, he had majored in philosophy, routinely questioning everything. He would pause briefly when challenged with a new idea, then methodically analyze its probability.

My father was a rare breed of philosopher in a nation that seemed to applaud industry and corporate endeavours at any cost to the environment. Debating philosophically with my father was a delightful change from the solitude of the prairies. My face turned red and voice rose while arguing gun control policy, but he always came through with the voice of reason.

We savoured facts, and statistics that could be proven inconclusive. My father and I were both coffee-sipping academics who enjoyed mental games and intellectual debate. We were fascinated by the subject of social norms. He was uncontrollable, spoke his mind, and always found excuses for investigation. Prefering analyzing, I often remained quiet. Wanting to view his research, I neglected my own. He was brilliant, and I lived in his academic shadow. I visited every couple of months, and on the first morning of every arrival, he would lay at least two maps on the kitchen table to study. It vexed him that I might waste gas or take the least efficient route.

When I told him the Trans-Canada highway was faster than the Number Sixteen Highway from Saskatoon to Thunder Bay, he dragged his laptop to double check. Like Corilene, I realized my father had to be right, willing to argue just to hear his children concede. He was annoyingly thorough and, most often, correct. His advice always saved me gas money, and the lunches he packed for the trip home reminded me that I was still his cherished daughter.

Now my father stumbled into the kitchen, his hair reminding me of textbook pictures of Sir Winston Churchill. He asked, with interest, what I was up to. Ex-police officers rarely shake their inquisitive nature. I told him that I was perplexed about some of the interviews I had with local and federal policemen regarding Saskatoon gangs. I outlined what I had learned in my interviews: there are apparently three basic reasons Aboriginal youth join gangs. He gazed at the microwave, waiting for his coffee, before responding to an argument that would require thought and Socrates-like reasoning skills.

Luring him into debate, I explained how young Aboriginals join city gangs because of poverty on the reserve. More than 70 percent are under the poverty line, with old skills of survival lost. I reminded my father that many of them lived in one-bathroom houses, increasing the danger of tuberculosis , a Third World disease that our citizens are still fighting. Often by the time residents on the reserve see a doctor on "doctors' day," their disease has progressed enough to warrant a hospital stay. Elders conceal their own illnesses, because they are interrupted by professionals who will not listen to the stories leading up to their ailments. Despite available immunizations, not all residents will stand in line for their shots.

## The Debate

Youth have no programs to keep them busy, no jobs to reward industriousness. They are paid to remain quiet, encouraged by their circumstances to achieve little. In the city, disdain meets them. They are labelled "ignorant" and shunned because they do not understand simple bus routes. They may then isolate themselves to avoid ridicule, and social workers must intervene to encourage them on their quest for better jobs and schooling. Although I shared my heart with a man who probably arrested young gang members when he was on the force, I suggested their reasons for crime were somewhat justifiable.

Reserve schools had limited funding. Teachers were expected to focus on math and English. In a land where snow held stubbornly to the land, outdoor activities were postponed until spring. They endured years of schooling taught in a second language, drained by the hunger and fatigue of malnutrition. Unless the band submitted a proposal with the Chief-in-Council in Prince Albert, few extra-curricular activities inspired them to undertake projects that would expand their understanding of their land. After school, children walked around the reserve with friends, avoiding houses made musty from mould. Houses with one bathroom and multiple inhabitants produce moisture conducive to the growth of mould. Once discovered, owners are instantly evacuated and the house burned to the ground – adding to the cycle of hopelessness. A real home is a place of refuge and safety, not a building that can be destroyed on little notice.

When gang leaders enter the reserve to recruit, disillusioned youngsters are eager to embrace a new life. Residents, too fearful to report the gang presence, disdainfully whisper amongst themselves. It is an unacknowledged awareness. New recruits often consent because their families in the city are being threatened by the gangs, or because it gives the abandoned ones a sense of belonging. Gang leaders, rarely executing the crime themselves, embrace naïve delinquents who will take the fall. If discovered revealing secrets, recruits suddenly go missing during a stroll in the woods. Once respected, elders can no longer protect their children's innocence.

My father, eager for debate, often interrupted me

as I argued my point. Both passionate, we could escalate a simple discussion to an ideological screaming match within minutes. Reminiscing about late '60's, he described reservation duty as draining. Even on dry reserves, evenings exploded with inebriation and passionate disputes between partners. He and his partner arrived on the scene to break up domestic violence. If it were simply the recruiting by gang members that caused crime, there would only be break-and-enters, which most gang crime entails. Removing guns from the hands of criminals was a simplistic answer to the cycle of addiction tormenting our young people.

My father delighted in arguing with me, and in playing devil's advocate.

The more I spoke of gang crime, the more he rebutted with family violence percentages. He had been on the calls, held violent men on the floor while handcuffing them, and his answers were based on experience, not academic theories. History just seems to repeat itself, he said.

"However," he paused, "back then most of us police officers were poor farm kids before entering the force where we earned a lower wage than they make now, so our level of empathy was much higher for the disadvantaged. It is easier for someone who understands poverty to sympathize with the drunken frustration of "not enough." We could understand and feel for their living situation," he sighed.

I glared at him as he licked peanut butter from his knife, praying the good Lord would spare me of that genetic habit. His opinion sounded socialistic, yet he seemed convinced that the police have now joined the academics. As their wages increased, so did their loyalty to the wealthy few who make the decisions. Picking up runaway children from residential schools where those children had been abused was not a favourite pastime for police officers. The very act bred mistrust toward the officers who must send them back to the Catholic schools. Perceived as enablers of a life of abuse, they too gained the reputation of abusers. Children were called savages, yet expected to trust a community who mistreated and disrespected them.

## Fatherhood

My father washed the dishes, watching the birds and thinking, reluctant to cause a genuine argument. Arguments were flaming arrows that pierced my heart. His arguments were painful, oral weapons that penetrated the flesh and left me questioning my ideals and beliefs. As a philosopher, his role in society was to challenge agendas. Yet he would not easily back down from an argument close to his heart.

Out on a call, he had missed my birth, sacrificing this important moment to rescue inebriated couples. His marriage weakened from the irregular shift work, and his children missed him each evening he was not there to read stories. He gained his wisdom through sacrifice. His years investigating criminals were reduced to social policing, yet he had the eyes of a father and the heart of a community builder. He understood the complexities of rebuilding a home abandoned by evacuation.

His goal that afternoon was to debate all aspects of the law and society regarding Aboriginal youth. His enlightenment was not drawn from newspaper articles alone. His political argument was not based on the Saskatoon newspaper's article about the two frozen babies and the lack of prosecution. His attention to detail and evidence earned him credibility. He had learned to prepare for a case and finish with excellence and clarity.

Aggravated by his case-building, I argued that gangs are created to make money from robbery and drugs. Television programs seen in the North appeal to young social deviants. There is big money from gang activity in Canada and little risk of prosecution. In the United States, drug possession has higher consequences; young people caught possessing narcotics go to jail for two years. In Canada, young offenders face little jail time. Canadian youth copy American gang colours, yet do not experience equivalent prosecution. Our court systems offer "benefits" for criminals.

"This is serious, Father," I clamoured, as though he were deliberately ignoring me. "I know you don't live on the prairies but it is a national issue!"

"No, what is serious," he parried, "is that police no longer have empathy for the disadvantaged. It used to be that police arrested criminals who committed crimes. They analyzed a situation for what it was. Now they are calling any inconvenience criminal behaviour. That is far more serious than gangs, granted, and scary because they are random perpetrators with a deliberate vengeance."

Kids who are annoying and demanding have sometimes been labelled deviant. Not all young people who look like punks are punks. Not all young Aboriginal people are part of a gang. Some are simply fatherless children seeking attention. They need people who will believe in them and challenge their minds.

"Laziness will hurt our society more than political parties ever will," he said. "If a foreign man from Eastern Europe looks suspicious in a Vancouver airport, tazer him. Impatient professionals teach young people that the inconvenient person in our society must die. Children and people can be inconvenient. That simply means we, as fathers, roll up our sleeves and work with them."

Young people on reserves are crying out for wisdom from their elders. They are crying out to be led by credible leaders, not sasquatches – chiefs who live in the city instead of their reservations. My companions were simply tried by society for being *inconveniences.* Frustrated by the hatred, they progress to criminal acts that earn real jail time. *Why strive for purification, when the toys of the middle class have left them empty? Why engage in a lifeless community?*

Realizing that my father was more patient than I remembered growing up, I recalled his attending our school functions, reading to us every night after supper, teaching us to listen to his voice of reason. Working with us to complete our homework, he was an involved parent. Engaging in our future, he worked harder as we grew more argumentative. He had been patient with the belligerent people in our neighbourhood, and meant what he said. Through his actions, we understood his belief in community policing. These words had been a catch phrase coined by sociology majors who suggested police officers on reserves and in tough neighbourhoods should build relationships and earn the trust of the residents.

Wanting to end our argument, I agreed that community policing would work. Apparently, crime decreases when police live on the reserve and become a part of the community. The most valuable aspect of the police-citizen relationship was lost when the British created treaties. Once trust was gone – it was difficult to rebuild and maintain. Rebuilding it would require the active participation of the community and the police. It would be worthwhile and the results would be long-term and far-reaching.

As I listened to my strong father sitting there, I began to believe that positive results were possible. A benefit of having a hard-working and honest father was knowing I could trust his word. The fatherless, robbed of this stability, were in a constant state of chaos. Strength is revived in coming home to visit a father, regardless of the past. For gang punks with no real home and having no one to trust, there is no trust. Like Peter Pan's lost boys, they are frozen in time.

## Healing

I was excited when my father hollered up the stairs for me to hurry. Although he was often impatient with how much time I spent curling my hair, he generally endured these female necessities with calm. Looking at the suede boots that made my jeans look sexy, he shook his head, complaining how useless those boots were for the wet wintry weather in northern Ontario. In the cool dry prairie winters, I argued, suede keeps frost at bay. I loved those boots, even if they did prove to my father I needed his travel advice. Looking at my unbuttoned jacket, he lowered his head with complete scorn for my lightweight ski jacket. Why hadn't I chosen something practical like a parka with big furry mittens?

He slipped on the icy sidewalk and I quickly reached out to grab him. Kicking snow off his shoe, he assured me he was fine. My heart sank. *Winters are getting harder on him*, I thought. He had been tough throughout the years, walking to his nightshift even in blizzards because we did not have a vehicle. He had a dream that his children would attend college; living without a vehicle would save enough money to fulfil that dream. Calling out, "Good night!" he pulled on his sturdy parka and funny-looking hat that rarely matched. His jacket was colourful so that the cars would see him. Once he had been hit by a car that quickly drove away, leaving him lying on the road with a broken leg, not stopping to help an aging man who was walking in the bitter cold so that one day his children could attend college.

He never complained, only reminded us how valuable reading was. We saw how books gave him joy and how his face would light up as he read *The Greatest Christmas Pageant Ever* – in the middle of summer. We only heard how his leg would heal quickly enough because he was a fighter.

He also attended classes when he had time, receiving honour marks for essays written with wisdom and experience. Still, he made time to attend my figure skating competitions. By example, he encouraged us to achieve our dreams. He was my father, and I was happy to follow him.

He knew that I was a daughter who needed answers. He simply waited for me to ask.

"Were you racist, Dad?" I whispered, "a '*gang punk*,' like the chiefs accuse you and other fathers of being?"

"Yep," he quickly replied. Seeing my confusion, he

eyed me with compassion. His pale blue eyes faded to gray as his voice softened. "They made us leave our own families to work overtime. Over 70 percent of the calls were domestic violence – regarding native people who were often drunk. When we got there, we would see holes in the walls of the house the government had built for them. Even though there was wood chopped in the back yard for their stoves, they would cut down their own walls instead of walking outside for wood. It was not racism, as much as it was frustration. Who were we to break up a domestic dispute when most of us were failing at our own marriages?"

Sighing as we walked, he perceived that I needed more. He had not physically abused my mother, as so many others had. Yet he knew that violent crime was often the consequence of failed marriage. Domestic violence was a crime of passion, a moment when alcohol often impaired judgement. Wanting to understand him as he was, I strove to embrace his words without judging them. Desiring to know him better, I forgave our past relationship. Letting go of resentment for my mother's heartbreak, I needed him to know that *I was looking for him.*

"Back then, the wife had to press charges herself," he said. "Now the police can press charges, but back then few women would press charges against an abusive husband – whom they often loved. Unlike gangs, domestic crime is one of selfish rage or passion against a family member. It is not acceptable, but somehow more understandable. Gang crime, on the other hand, is about blatant rebellion and deliberate malicious behaviour. Their crime is so frightening because it is random and destroys strangers. The only thing that has changed is that the media exposes these experiences today and women speak out against domestic violence, so there is help. Few men want to know that a woman would really want to leave. Men still regret a marriage that isn't working."

Feeling guilty about needing to drive extra miles to interrogate him, I lowered my eyes. He and I had weathered storms few were willing to endure. Yet he was fearless about truth, real about pain. He missed his children, even through that hardened exterior. He missed his family, secretly longing for them to return home. Wisdom came at a price, and respect was gained by fathering throughout cold nights. Our moment of understanding brought back childhood memories of him cooking pancakes on Saturday morning for us, after a tiring night shift. I could smell the syrup.

Children on the reserve were learning to *play the game* by watching some of their elders attend bingo and stagger home. These perceptive students lost respect for a lifestyle once overlooked. Longing for a father to initiate family meetings at the kitchen table, children are battling with a pattern they are desperate to avoid. They want to return home, to sleep in a bed warmed by a kookum's quilt.

First Nations youth need to hear their fathers say, *I miss you.* He does not have to be perfect, only present. The stakes are higher now, because children want more. Lying in bed without a simple *goodnight* is lonely. It makes winters unbearable and summers troublesome.

## Chapter Nine

# Pas de

## *French Lit, 200.3*
## *Assignment #4*

## *Ma Mère Aimait Les Petits Enfants Autochtones*

*Par*
*Paula Henderson*

Je me rappelle bien, des étés que j'ai passés sur la réserve indienne à la station de santé avec ma mère, où elle avait été postée par le département de Santé. La boue était très profonde et je perdais souvent mes bottes dans la boue et je devais clapoter avec mes chaussettes. Être sur la réserve était non seulement difficile physiquement, mais aussi une merveilleuse leçon de survie. Les Autochtones étaient des gens tranquilles et introspectifs, qui développaient continuellement de nouvelles stratégies pour survivre. Ils étaient des artistes créatifs, qui pouvaient s'exprimer à ceux qui écouteraient. Cependant, ils cachaient toujours leur bouche quand ils souriaient parce qu'ils étaient très timides. Ma mère apprenait souvent les noms de tous les enfants et s'assurait qu'ils étaient en sécurité. Ils étaient comme ses propres enfants, et souvent elle était coupable de garder leurs chatons et cherchaient des bonbons dans ses poches de manteau.

Ma mère aimait les gens, et a grandi surtout très attachée à tous les petits enfants comme s'ils étaient les siens. Elle était très protectrice, et les aimait comme une mère poule. Donc c'était naturel pour elle de demander au Chef et aux gens de la clinique de santé de se débarrasser des chiens sauvages qui couraient partout sur la réserve. Elle craignait les dommages que les chiens sauvages causaient sur la réserve. La bande ne voulait pas abattre les chiens, parce que culturellement ils n'aiment pas tuer sans raison, et le gouvernement ne s'implique pas dans les problèmes qui ne sont pas nécessairement politiques. Le Prêtre n'intervenait pas quand il y avait un problème, à moins d'être religieusement nécessaire c'est mieux de ne pas créer un conflit entre les religions protestante, catholique et autochtone.

Une fois pendant que ma mère me rendait visité, nous avons reçu un appel téléphonique. Je remercie Dieu car elle a entendu les mauvaises nouvelles pendant qu'elle était avec moi. Les chiens errants avaient attaqué et mordu une petite fille sur la réserve que ma mère connaissait et avait chérie. La petite fille était morte durant l'attaque et les chiens avaient mangé la moitié de son corps. Ma mère est allée dans sa chambre et a regardé par la fenêtre, quand elle a entendu les nouvelles. Elle avait un chagrin dans les yeux qu'aucune femme chrétienne ne devrait avoir. Ma mère est une personne très forte, mais ce jour-là je l'ai vue complètement effondrée. Ce ne sont pas les Chefs qui souffrent dans cette nation, ni les Politiciens canadiens. Ce ne sont pas les prêtres catholiques qui souffrent dans cette nation, ni les Pasteurs Protestants. Les enfants sont ceux qui pleurent parce qu'ils sont torturés. La mort de cette petite fille est passée complètement inaperçu dans les médias, pourtant chaque mort sur une réserve indienne devrait rendre la nation entière honteuse.

# Chapter Ten

# 9/11

# Investigation

The snow crunched beneath my feet, and air ripped through my lungs. The white sea on either side of the unplowed road acted as a buffer between me and the forest, which was notorious for swallowing locals. Warned in the summer there was quicksand in the bush, I was convinced that more dangers lurked between those trees in the heart of winter. Placing my boots carefully as I walked, I noticed the orange sun lowering to greet the tops of the towering spruce trees. The evening was calm, and in the North, daylight ends abruptly at five p.m. Marching quickly, a sense of urgency overwhelmed me as I strove to reach the store before the night fell. The bush is eerie in the black night, as wailing winds tear through the shrubs like ghosts.

Arctic wind froze together my eyelids. Wincing occasionally I suddenly saw two little children follow me into the ditch. The little girls with choppy brown hair followed me down the road to the one store on the reserve. Matching my pace, they joined me with little explanation. I could not figure out how they knew me, but then remembered I was the *white girl*, with high cheekbones and height that intimidated most of them. Like a puzzle laid out on a table, their quiet investigation quickly pieced together which family I belonged to. They reminded me of a gentler homeland security team, created after 9/11.

Much to my chagrin they tugged at my jacket, pushing me closer to the ditch. At first I thought they were being belligerent, when suddenly a pick-up truck zoomed by at 75 miles an hour. *WHOOOOOSH.* Thankful, I engaged the vivacious children in conversation. They were well-kept little girls, with shiny black hair, flimsy winter coats and no mittens. I was amazed at their resistance to the weather. Then I remembered that most families on the reserve receive less than ten thousand a year on social assistance. Trying to keeping a home heated at minus 50 sucks up a lot of grocery and clothing money.

*Whoosh.* Angry at the trucks, I asked the girls to explain to me why they were driving so fast. I had been on the unpaved road, where locals had died, and feared the road myself. Unfortunately, the children on the reserve were familiar with death. They had seen casualties, like skidoos falling into icy lakes, and cars being crushed by moose. Protecting me from the dangers of the woods, they were walking with me to the store in case I became lost or worse.

I asked them about their Christmas, and what they expected. They told me how excited they were to have their very own shampoo and conditioner for Christmas. Although they did not leave the reserve, the girls announced that they could access the computers at the school. Studying me, like a character in a science fiction movie, they asked if I had my own email address in Saskatoon. Feeling indignant, I assured the girls that my city in the flatlands was just as *global* as the *oil patch* communities. We, too, have Internet, and watched the global village mourn over terrorist attacks. Even though the children are isolated, television updates them despite government gag orders censoring events on the reserves. Just as I began my explanation, another push from the girls sent me into the ditch once again.

*WHOOOOOOSH*, another truck soared past, almost nicking my jacket as it zipped threw the snow.

Although Aboriginal children are often giddy and full of life, they speak few words. When they do speak, their words resonate. As one girl tilted her head, she pondered which words she should use, then with a surge of courage told me that I would be run over by a truck. My coat was long and white, and my hat was not suitable for extreme winter conditions. Since I had not seen the last two trucks soar by like hawks, I handed over my care to my escorts.

With big cat like eyes they asked what I was doing for Christmas, and why I would need to go the store when my mother had so much food in the fridge. I had to explain my addiction for chips. They did not quite understand that if I did not need chips, why I would worry about them. They suggested that, instead of losing weight by walking down the road, maybe I should just eat fewer chips. They giggled, clasping hands over their mouths because they did not like people to see the stained teeth behind their smiles. Their laughter was enchanting.

The average small town grocery store is over two hours away. Unless a young mother raising a baby at the average age of sixteen has family with a truck, there are no shopping sprees. The children wear clothes purchased from garage sales, and skate on mini ice rinks made by their fathers. On some reserves, toddlers play in backyards, near garbage piled high enough for overhead planes to see. There is no garbage pick-up. Every convenience city people take for granted is a luxury on a reserve, especially on an isolated reserve.

## Celebration

I had come that winter to help with Christmas programs. However, I mostly sat in the rocking chair, eating turkey, amused by my mother's kittens. Free of social obligations, I meandered throughout the duplex, placing bowls of icing and decorations at each of the *cooking* stations set up on the tables.

"What do you do first?" I could hear my mother call, as more teens arrived.

"Wash our hands," they giggled, and walked quickly to the washroom.

Not all families on the reserves could afford baking supplies. For the teens, baking hot cookies and icing them was a treat. Christmas, in general, was often looked upon with anticipation and excitement. It was not just a time for presents, but there was a supper at the school. The Catholic church offered midnight mass, while children wearing brand new embroidered mittens giggled in the pews. It was a time when the community remembered family, and visited neighbors each evening. Entertaining guests was a winter vacation pastime.

Aboriginal youths seemed disinterested in the lessons of *old culture*. Instead, they were enamored by rock videos, television, "hanging out" in town or on another reserve. Until they became parents and realized they were unable to cook, the value of the old cultural ways was overlooked. Nor did they see how limited social assistance cheques were—not seeing their own parents often unable to afford blankets and clothing for their children. Gladly they arrived at my mother's residence, hoping to learn the basic art of creating sugar cookies. Their eyes shone upon seeing the different colors of icing. Intrigued by the tortilla shells I had on the counter, they insisted that I show them what a quesadilla was. They puckered as they tasted salsa for the first time.

The young women blossomed as they created crafts. Knowing that the government is not always the solution when children are without blankets to keep them warm at night, my mother developed a cooking and quilting class on Friday evenings. Expecting few to be interested, she was pleasantly surprised by how quickly her basement filled with women eager and delighted to sew clothes for their babies.

Wanting to revive the skills of a culture lost, they worked hard to learn crafts. The moccasin slippers an elder had made for me were beaded with perfection, truly a treasure to look at and study in detail. Made of leather, they smelled of the wilderness, rustic yet delicate. Near the toe lay a large rose with leaves in green, with a white and gold background made with delicate beads. Veteran ability was evident by how perfect the design lay, and how close together the beads were. Not one stitch was visible, not one mistake evident.

Years of culture, experience and tradition blended into these treasures. Yet the tradition was disappearing, and my mother was one of the few to encourage skills. Unable to teach moose tufting, it was evident that she alone was not enough. Had the Aboriginals been encouraged to sell to people off reserve in the past, my moccasins would now not be my cherished antiques.

The girls spent evenings laying out squares on the

floor, yelling at the cats to stop running over them, snagging thread on their paws. They laughed to see the cats chase threads caught on their tails. What truly mattered was that they were with an older woman who cared—a Cree *wannabe*—they called her. She was a role model, who realized that practical teaching develops young girls into women. They were a community, and needed an elder to teach the skills they were missing. Instead, they had been left through the decades to raise themselves, hopelessly dependent.

Often the mothers, who should have been teaching daughters how to survive, were drinking, recovering from the pain of residential schools. Seeing their quilts stretched out on the racks, women crawled out of the pit of discouragement. Accomplishing simple tasks helped the frustrated women to develop problem-solving skills. They were becoming capable and appreciated.

The youth enjoyed the cooking classes, and became empowered at the same time. Starting with spaghetti and meat sauce, they finished with cabbage rolls. Many had been caught up in the lifestyle of cooking canned goods, purchasing whatever was sold at the store. One did not shop for health, but according to budget. Once they learned how to make an evening meal on a limited budget, they could conceptualize the benefits of healthy eating.

Subsidized houses built on reserves were nippy. Children without those quilts would shiver all through the night. Wood stoves warmed a room slightly, but smoke attacked their eyes. Asking for a snack, some of the children informed me their only meal had left them hungry. Bologna sandwiches and apples were a common staple during the week. Cringing, I remembered too as a child, pressing together two pieces of white bread with only mustard in the middle. For years, we *pretended* we had sandwich meat. Trying to keep the fridge door closed, I grabbed cheese and apples for the kids, hoping to remove the stain of guilt. Our fridge had become full over the years; but we had not forgotten the shame of begging.

The malnourished children attended school where they were obligated to focus on tasks in a language that was not their own. At least the school was warmer than their houses. All government buildings were required to maintain reasonable heat during winter. If the children did not go to school, social services could remove them from their homes. Parents wanted to keep their family intact, and so insisted that the children attend school even if they were late.

The further north they live, the more sunlight residents have during summer, and the less during the winter. During the spring and summer, there are only four hours of dark to let children know that it is bedtime. In winter, after months of twelve hours days of darkness, all of the residents are vitamin D deficient, and those without a supplemental diet including milk or vitamins become unwell.

## Welcome to Politics

Happy to return home where I could raise the thermostat as high as I wanted, I nestled back into my routine. Preparing for another semester of university, I quickly erased from my mind my depression over the north. Other students were dumbfounded when I stated that I had returned from the *Canadian shantytowns*. Some of the housing reminded me of pictures seen in war movies, but not all of the communities were disgruntled. Many northern residents were content with the simple lifestyle, unaware that they lived well below poverty levels. The younger generation, raised on television, succumbed to the materialism of my generation. Now expensive running shoes and designer jeans were important.

After returning home from my Christmas vacation, it was easy to get refocused on my college classes, and the hassle of bill paying. Purchasing textbooks, and a coffee for the long line up I would have to endure, became a much more daunting task. Remembering the children who suggested I eat fewer cookies, I giggled. Their sweetness infringed on my need to be *neutral.* They were not my problem and, as long as I kept quiet about my views, life would be simpler. Although they had seemed to snuggle into a heart that had been as ice cold as the lake they skated on, I quickly forgot their plight when I returned to evenings of study and work. I tried to tell myself, when my mother called, that her *issues* were the consequence of working on an isolated reserve. It was her choice to live there; Aboriginal politics were of little concern to my own political views.

"I was asked by management if I were being more loyal to the First Nations people than to them," she wept in disbelief over the phone.

"What?" I asked flabbergasted. "Your manager is not allowed to inquire about your personal political beliefs! For goodness sake, skirts were created for Mennonite girls joining cadets, Sikh policemen can wear turbans, yet your loyalty is questioned because you helped First Nations people make quilts? Seriously,

Mother, only a communist would think those kinds of questions are acceptable!"

Thinking her plight was that simple, I convinced her to forgive the blatant ignorance.

In the city, *neutrality* in Canada is self-serving, disguised as company loyalty. It is a concept that keeps the middle class content despite human suffering. As long as voters do not see the consequences of their neutrality, they remain guiltless over the deaths of little children eaten by wild dogs on First Nations reserves.

Loyalty was rarely a demand placed on city dwellers living a fast-paced life. Many were more consumed with their own comfort than the plight of the First Nations peoples in the city. If First Nations people were given a job in the city, they were expected to work. Urban employees were not required to like or dislike people based on their race. *Respect and dignity* is written on all the signs, hanging on the walls of the hospitals. Yet in the north, the request for respect is surreal. First Nations men reveal their suture scars, and believe it normal to see a paramedic rather than nurse practitioner for overtime calls.

Thinking of our phone call; I vaguely remembered meeting with a representative at Indian Affairs. Wanting statistics to aid my research for a public administration paper during my senior year of college, I was allowed to ask questions on "Aboriginal" costs to the province and the federal government. Hoping to understand the cutbacks, I was trying to be thorough in my understanding of the actual spending. Hearing professionals complain about government waste, I was curious as to whether we really were *picking up the tab* for Aboriginal people. *Were they a burden*? Why would everyone involved in the *care industry* be so cautious? Were they really a "minority" receiving "majority" benefits, or were the allegations simply a "playing card" in the game of politics? It seemed apparent to me that the probable solution for all situations was "neutral ground", where everyone speaks about nothing, then regrets the lack of quality the relationship has produced. Quality relationships are only developed through communication, and understanding only achieved with honesty.

As the bus passed the many little towns on my way to Regina, I became aware that there was no real frame of reference. Should I compare the spending to the general population? Or compare the supply with demand? It was then that I realized it is a matter of public perception. Farmers would not be angry if the federal government helped them out during a drought; rather, they would be delighted with their good fortune. Unions Employees would not be angry by increased wages. Any low and middle income family would welcome an increase in the Child Tax Benefit. As I stepped off the bus, I reminded myself that the real political debate is not about how much, but to whom. To whom is the tax dollar being allocated?

I remembered the meeting well, because I was offered horrible coffee with stale-tasting powdered cream. The government representative shut the door behind him, signaling that he could be a while. His eyes were soft after years of conversing, but his resolve stern. Polite, desiring to enlighten me, he spoke methodically. *Was that a political deflection maneuver, forcing aspiring intellects to pay the price for legitimate research* I wondered.

Reviewing the list of expenses, it occurred to me that there will always be a fight provincially and federally over who pays for the monstrous cost of health care spending in the cities and reserves. As long as Aboriginal people are on the reserves, their funding is federal; once Aboriginals enter the city, health care costs become the responsibility of the provincial government. Aboriginals who live in the cities are covered by provincial health care, and therefore by provincial taxation. They pay taxes on their cheques like everyone else with a job. When they work on reserve, their wages are tax-free. Tax-free wages are meant as an incentive to return to the reserve, to establish role models for the youth. Job shortages with their associated unemployment and increased need for social assistance on reserves are no incentive for generational change.

I asked the bureaucrat to show me where financial costs were the highest. I was overwhelmed, realizing more money was spent on the judicial system for crimes committed by Aboriginal youth than most assets they owned per capita. At the time, youth crime had grown by over 300 percent. It never occurred to me to analyze the progressive steps to becoming a social deviant or a permanent jail cell resident. Although many locals did not understand these political playing cards, they did understand increases in crime. Provincial residents were well aware of wait times in emergency rooms. Politics are not disguised in the daily life of residents driving past courthouses. The consequences of public policy are all around us.

Mulling over the statistics upon my return, it became evident why a social worker had advised me that the crime rate is an indicator of social dysfunction. I had witnessed the same cultural dysfunction, regardless of the size of the community, finally perceiving that it started on reserves. Technology and materialism had influenced First Nations young people, just as it had in the city. Many escaped the reserves to find a better life, like other rural children. Our ideals as a nation deviated as quickly as the local and global markets shifted. First Nations youth are simply a displaced people struggling to find a home.

## Let It Shine

My mother had seen the dysfunction of the reserves escaped; she recognized the benefits for the unskilled to have a project in hand to create production. She knew, as an elder, that the younger must learn from the older and wiser. They must learn from the women and men who had walked their journey and learned from their mistakes. It is the simplest teachings that produce the greatest results. As a mother makes a quilt with love, her strength grows in knowing she can protect her child. It is the responsibility of all the people to build a community which values hospitality.

Role models are imperative for Aboriginal youth facing modern issues. Without a home, they don't learn the basics. Children wander the reserve, blissfully unaware of time constraints. Bedtime is unimportant in a land with constant light, and few rules confine the children. In the city, they are unaccustomed to protocol like phoning in to work to say they are not coming. With technological changes, they became accustomed to microwavable food despite the cost.

Each time I visited, more and more quilts had been completed. Smiling children raced home with crafts. During one of the youth nights, I could see how the mothers were relieved to discover how to make large meals with simple health-improving recipes on a tight budget. Rebuilding confidence comes from small victories. Reservation dwellers do not have the same opportunity to buy groceries as city dwellers. Vegetables are scarce; milk is double the cost of what it is off reserve.

The young children so enjoyed their classes that they began to learn the songs that my mother sang while I was growing up. She hummed softly as she cooked, not realizing how important those melodies were. One day while watching a video of the children taped by a teacher, she noticed that the children were singing her songs. They did not miss a beat, word or rhythm. They instinctively appreciated music. They were not just able to remember the words, but the actions too, singing Sunday school songs as though they led the choir.

She was so surprised by her unintentional influence that tears began to roll down her cheeks. "Those stinkers," she mused. "They look like they are not paying attention, yet they remember every word." She began to think that it would be a wonderful idea if they could sing at the school Christmas program. They all agreed, hands flying into the air, hoping that she would choose them to sing. She assured them if they attended practices at the school she could help them perfect a song of their choice. The excited children chose *This Little Light of Mine,* an old church chorus. They loved that song, mostly because they got to stop their friends, with finger and mouth actions, from *blowing their candle out.* Sometimes their light would keep flickering, but an occasional kid would get too passionate about blowing at a pretend candle and spit. Trying to avoid a brawl, my mother would raise her hands with new actions to distract the older chubby child from punching the spitter.

Until children appeared on stage, my mother had been concerned some of them might cry. No one did as she handed out real candles, warning the children not to singe anyone's hair or eyebrows. Gliding on the stage with candles lit, they sang until all of the people in the gym were mesmerized by their intense faces. *This little light of mine*, they sang in unity, *I'm going to let it shine. I won't let Satan blow it out* they chimed loudly.

Their confidence was a proud moment for the teachers and helpers who had invested in those scruffy looking children that now stood tall. Although children seemed at times uninterested, they were listening, observing and learning. They were auditory learners, often remembering words through song, and enjoying a love of music that radiates from their eyes with a sweet, uncontaminated joy. Their little lights will shine everyday, not even extinguished by the ill wind of political issues.

I found it ironic that, although these kids were on an isolated reserve, through their school Internet they learned they were part of the global village. They could see different regions of the world by watching the screen. Each had his or her own encounter with the non-Aboriginal people also. They knew which professionals genuinely cared, and which were simply caught up in a career. When they entered town restaurants, they also understood who welcomed them.

In fact, they seemed to have a greater appreciation for world perspectives than their focus toward federal or provincial politics. They were First Nations people who identified as with their own nation. The only thing that the Internet could not teach them was how to build a home. Agencies built houses; but very few created homes.

I remember the morning of 9/11 and all of the phone calls that followed. Panicked, I phoned north to ensure my mother was safe. Everyone was stunned, watching the television in silence. They could empathize with a nation attacked for their political beliefs. They understood the dividing line between national loyalties. We are the only nation that has convinced ourselves that the prolonged misunderstanding of a minority race is acceptable.

One of her co-workers came to comfort my mother. United in fear, both races sat stunned, unsure if this was the destructive blow that would render an undefeated nation helpless. All employees were eventually asked to go home, in the event that Canada too was a target of war.

Although isolated, First Nations people could identify very quickly with the pain of losing a home and a country. Victims of their own domestic war, they grieved with those who mourned. They were not savages and they were very much up to date about world politics. Through the media, First Nations people have been able to grasp global perspective, in and amongst their own cultural experience. Like the brown horse, they are merely isolated. As I watched replays of the Twin Trade Towers crumbling on the television, I understood why the horse wandered. He was wild, yet trapped by boundaries. He was free, yet lonely in an abandoned town. He was wise, yet becoming obsolete.

## Chapter Eleven

# He Scores!

## The Scrappy Scrapbooker

Glory's departure left me without an outlet for my creativity. Abandoned in the prairies, I was over 30 and bored. As I slipped back into the vortex of working at the hospital and paying bills, my projects and social life began to deteriorate. Thrilled that my neighbour Brenda had invited me over to make a scrapbook, I dragged my "project box" out of the closet. Being creative with many projects on my mind, I simply needed a catalyst for finishing an idea. Photos, given to me by friends and family, sat in the box, representing years of life missed while trying to build a career. The camera my sister gave me remained idle. During a visit, I offered it to Glory who had a young family. She was religious about capturing precious moments, and I was happy to bless her for returning home to Saskatchewan, reminding us we were still remembered.

Two of Saskatoon's most popular hobbies are watching the hockey game and scrapbooking. Whenever I walked past Brenda's apartment, I saw collages of photos on her wall, which made me regret all the special moments missed with my own family. Unique and creative, Brenda displayed her love and affection on that wall. Often as I strolled past their first floor patio, I saw Brenda scrapbooking while her husband JR watched the hockey game. As he sipped his soda, their little daughter pranced around the living room, relishing the hugs he would give when she came too close. They were Saskatchewan soul mates who enjoyed married life.

Learning from a mutual friend that Brenda was a veteran scrapbooker, I was eager to draw upon her experience. I loved how ordinary pictures turned into pages of cherished memories. The project capturing her college graduation was especially intriguing. While I mooched quarters for my laundry, I noticed how she stood so proudly in those photos. In our complex, Brenda was known for her preparedness and her organization. She had conquered life and seized her dreams. Tiny yet mighty, her dark, penetrating eyes hid behind funky retro glasses that revealed her humour. High cheekbones and silky black hair spoke of her Aboriginal descent. Often pulled into a ponytail, her hair bounced as she walked. Although appearing to be reserved, she was quite spunky. When I battled her for the clothes dryer, she would charm me into letting her use it first.

As I sauntered down the hallway stairs towards her basement suite, Brenda stood at the door, waiting for me. This career woman and mother was also a hardcore scrapbooker, putting fear and intimidation to those with less creativity. In her apartment, the bright colors and artistic displays were almost overwhelming. I sank into a kitchen chair, glancing about with trepidation. Seeing the sandwich bag of photos in my hand, she quickly assessed me as a wanna-be. Her husband smiled from the couch at my rapid loss of innocence, as she grabbed a black waist-high wheeled toolbox. It was apparently full of weapons.

Looking at me like a hit man, Brenda informed me

that scrapbooking is intense. Intimidated by the arsenal, my imagination took over. She drew open four drawers, like something out of a James Bond movie. *She is one of the Bond girls,* I told myself. On closer inspection, I saw buttons, ribbons, paper, enough glue sticks to get her through the apocalypse, and sandpaper. I studied all these expensive tools, my lips trembling. JR smiled indulgently at her, as if he had just seen a hat trick in the hockey game. He took personal joy seeing his wife intimidate aspiring young artists who dared enter her underground world. Even their little girl wiggled with delight in her chair as she saw her mommy begin. Even their little girl wiggled with delight in her chair as she saw her mommy begin; and all the while was assembling her own little toddler necklace, aspiring to be like her hero. Not even the fluffy, soft-pawed kitten could distract the two hardcore artisans.

"We ordered pizza," said JR. "You are welcome to have some." He was still grinning; he knew I was going to be there awhile. I was thankful for their hospitality, and eager to get started. Brenda winced at the sight of the sandwich baggie photos.

"Uh, I have a plan," I assured her.

"What is it?" she said with skepticism.

"I am going to use my blue paper," I explained nonchalantly.

"And what are you going to put with it?" she asked with an undertone of doubt.

Ordinarily I was very confident. As a writer, I had succumbed to neurotic coffee drinking habits and even wore a candy penguin in the ski pass flap of my winter coat. On occasion I was less than organized but now I was somewhat offended by her interrogation. Seeking support in the emotional minefield, I looked to JR. The game had ended and he now had his nose in a newspaper, occasionally glancing proudly at his wife. He seemed smitten by her, even though she had told me in the laundry room that they had been together for years. He strove to make tender eye contact to remind her that he was intoxicated and maintained the wide-eyed innocence only true love brings. Embarrassed, she gave him a small smile, acknowledging with a quick tip of her head that she was thankful for his undeserved adoration.

As the two innocently flirted, I was taken aback by their outward expression. Generally, First Nations people from the reservation use few facial expressions. Yet JR appeared to defy all stereotypes. He was openly affectionate and for no particular reason brought her presents. Passers-by witnessed their contentment as they sat on the couch holding each other, watching television. We all enviously inhaled the aroma of steaks barbecuing on the grill. They were happy – and happy with each other. On the mantle of the fireplace, stood more photos and a scrapbook project that JR had asked Brenda to create of their daughter.

"I am a writer you know," I reminded JR as he read.

"I know," he said with assurance.

"I really do think you should let me write about your wife and you," I insisted, as Brenda look at me with hesitation.

"Sure," he declared, "we have nothing to hide."

No, they did not hide their relationship, although Brenda was naturally more reserved than her husband. He was gregarious, with natural curls and rosy Santa cheeks. Although he was multi-faceted with natural leadership ability, the simplicity of love kept him calm. Their love was mystical, contrary to how the world perceives happiness. Often women dance with delight when they score another wage increase, or drive a shiny new vehicle. To make ends meet, JR and Brenda shared a basement apartment with her sister while attending school. Space was getting tight and the tension of wanting a house was high. One day a bank would approve them. They would purchase the starter home with a fence that every young family dreamed of.

The challenge that lay before me was creating a scrapbook page Brenda would approve of. I could literally see her nose twitching. *It is the markings of a veteran,* I thought. Sensing the need to appease her, I enlisted her help to pick out the right colors for the page. Leaning over to her box storing her weapons of choice, she quickly pulled out ribbon for the green page, stickers, buttons, and sandpaper for the photos I had obviously not cropped properly, and black ink to *lightly* dust the edges.

I had almost forgotten that I asked JR for his love story that wintry evening. I had badgered him, as a writer often does when digging for a story. It was so cold the following weeks that the roads were icy, and even the churches in the prairie Bible Belt cancelled services. I struggled to plug in my vehicle. It was so frozen I was afraid I would crack the bumper trying to plug in the cord. My fingers stung from the 45 below Celsius weather, even though my mittens were lined. My sweaty hospital scrubs were stained and crumpled due to a long, stressful cooking shift. My legs, unprotected by those flimsy hospital scrubs, began to shake as though my circulation was weakening. I wanted to cry I was so cold, but I knew that my eyelashes would just freeze together as they had before; and then it would take hours to regain proper focus. I ran to the front door of my apartment, and fumbled with my mittens to put the key into the lock.

I smiled with relief as the warm air rushed toward me in the apartment hallway. Hopping up the stairs to my apartment, I frantically searched for my keys again, cursing the northern winds and dreaming of soaking in a steaming bath. I could not bear to answer the phone, and did not relish having to change, wash the pile of dishes, and hang up the clothes I had recklessly thrown on my bedroom floor as I had rushed to get ready for work. I just wanted to lie on my bed and look at the ceiling with my winter coat on and boots still on my feet. Pushing open the door, the papers on the floor crinkled. Assuming they were announcements of ever-increasing rent in our booming city, I walked over them, deciding not to read the bad news until I changed into my favourite jeans and woolly sweater. I hated socks, yet had no choice but to don itchy, gray, wool socks. Feeling sorry for myself having to survive on my own, I meandered over to the coffee maker. Reaching for my favourite mug, I yelled at my cats to stop weaving in and out around my feet.

## The Journal

I discovered that the papers lying on my floor were nine typed pages of JR's love story. A little note in black marker read: "Sorry, I ran out of black ink." He had printed the entire story in light blue. He had actually done it – taken me seriously and written about his relationship. I have rarely met a man who could put into words how he felt about his wife. It was organized and worded like a journal. Part of me did not want to read the prose expressing his affection. Only a year earlier, I had heard those same words professed by a charming man who promised to love me eternally. I wanted to read books about how men are evil, and feel as though "thirty something" was electric. I would have died for the man that sent me the most beautiful flowers last Valentine's Day. Instead, on my shelf stood a vase with dried little roses and tiger lilies, reminding me that love is only temporary, only for fools who dream.

Lying on my kitchen table, the siren call of his words tempted me. I felt like a curious interloper snooping through someone else's mail. How could I let it just sit there for the "right time?" Isn't it always the "right time" to read the journal of a man who is madly and passionately in love? I savoured the papers, like a woman savouring chocolate. Slumping onto my chaise, I focused on the light blue words, my arm reaching out to grab the cappuccino cup that I thought was still half-full. Frustrated at the empty take-out cup, I still could not take my eyes off those papers. They were organized, meticulously detailed, and revealed the day his heart had been smitten. JR remembered the exact date of the journey's beginning. He knew the very moment he realized she was "the one." The first vulnerable words grabbed my attention, causing my breathing to become irregular. He had my full attention.

While reading this sweet love story, I groused, especially so near Valentine's Day. Jumping off the chaise with vexation, I threw the take-out cup in the garbage and reached for the coffee I had forgotten was brewing. I headed to the fridge for the half-and-half I bought religiously, along with my expensive, trendy, whole bean coffee. There was none. I had the entire evening to retreat under a warm, homemade quilt while enjoying a freshly brewed coffee and a personal journal – and I had no cream. I would conquer that story if it tortured me all evening. My cats looked at me, perplexed by my unfamiliar mood. The calico brought her green spongy ball (once dunked in the toilet) to my feet, hoping a game of fetch would cheer me up. I reminded her that playing fetch with the spongy ball mostly cheered her up; I had a story to read.

Carefully unfolding the papers, I began. JR commenced by describing how he first saw Brenda at the casino where they both worked. He was just working, hoping to earn a steady income. At that time, he had thought a little about his future, but his youthful excitement occupied most of his time. An outgoing prankster, he always engaged his friends – and strangers – in genuine conversation. JR was a people person, rarely at a loss for words. As Brenda strolled by, his heart was struck numb. He was unsure how to engage *her* in conversation. Her beauty made him nervous, and this spunky little woman working security intrigued him. She perplexed him. He later learned she was not someone who would be interested in a casual affair. She seemed to prance around, unaware and uninterested in his existence. She was different, and who could not help but gawk at her beauty.

Trying to impress her as the suave gentleman he believed he was, he teased her about being a security guard at her size. Teasing was what he knew how to do; it was how he showed affection to his family and friends.

After teasing her like a boy in a schoolyard, surely he would catch her attention and she would realize how witty and charming he was. Surely, his gregarious smile and innocent flirting would make her see that he was "into her," although she did not even know this tall, dark and handsome man's name.

She was not amused by his underestimation of her strength or that she took her employment and organizing skills seriously. Looking him in the eye, she reminded him that she could escort him out of the Casino. *Strike One* he wrote.

I giggled with delight because it reminded me of the country song *Swing Batter Batter.* I knew he would approach her from another angle after the first one failed. JR saw problems from more than one angle. She would soon warm to him as everyone else did.

I could perceive the frustration and dismay he felt trying to impress this woman. I felt sorry for JR because she had also intimidated me with her nonchalance. I envisioned S*trike Two* as he described the introduction from his brother that did nothing for her. He had been certain his easy-going brother would successfully tag team with him, convincing her that his smile was powerful enough to woo any woman. He did not realize that most women want more than a pretty boy. He was at a loss how he should approach the girl next. *What did she want or need?* he pondered. Desperate, he decided to befriend her, to discover what it is to love a woman sincerely.

Invited out to the bowling lane where their mutual friends would be, he took the opportunity to step up his game by shamelessly flirting with her, revealing his wit and showing off his sassy bowling shoes. *Strike Three* he wrote. Unlike other girls, she was not easily impressed. She left, mistakenly believing he was a player because he could not stop looking at some blonde girls in another alley. He swore they were old classmates he had not seen since high school. The night of bowling may have warmed her up, but it still did not produce any real attraction.

*"Wow,"* I mouthed sardonically, *"here in the prairies, bowling is a sure thing."*

I was now thoroughly intrigued as he went on to say how shocked he was by her indifference. Artistic and sensitive, her organizational skills intimidated others. Ponytail bouncing as she walked, she wanted to know what he meant by the word "interested." She had seen charm before, had known empty promises. Love had failed her, as it had many women. She had been bitten by life, yet, she wanted a man who would hold her while they watched the sunrise each morning. He needed to understand that she wanted a relationship she could come home to, a child who loved making crafts, and a house to decorate.

She was secretly sensitive – her spirit would break if he robbed her of hope. Knowing the casino was a short-term career, she applied to become a nurse's aid. Although she was ambitious, she was a natural caregiver who would not receive personal love and affection with ease. After a life of soothing the wounds of others, it would not be easy to take pleasure in the affection of someone so loud, so boisterous and so determined. His sanguine ease with adoration intimidated her. She was quiet, and revealed her kindness through actions. He represented a life of dreams coming true and feelings of security. Yet he also represented a life of surrender, sacrifice and risk that most avoid for self-protection.

On page four, JR bemoaned the fact that she was so hard to win over. Wooing her would require a more precise strategy. Striking up a conversation, he showed genuine interest in what she was doing and needed. He continued to tell her jokes and tease her, hoping to win her smile. He began to ache for that smile, and longed for her presence, even the mere presence of a quick phone call. Always in his thoughts, her spunky attitude revived his warmth. Her presence became his passion, fuelling the desire to one day hold her hand in the middle of the night while the wind howled about the rafters. He would build a relationship with security. He could see their future in her eyes, even though she responded with a skepticism that masked her fear.

Retreating is safe and becomes easier when a woman passes thirty. Opportunities lost simply become deep regrets and an excuse for disdain. Reading his story, I cheered for her to take that, as though she represented all who would die for a brief moment of tender love rather than endure years of cruel fantasy. Genuine affection and kindness unnerved her. She would have to see life in a different way, and see a future that would involve risk. She would have to allow her heartbeat to drown out the voices of reason and the bad memories consuming her.

One evening, becoming accustomed to Brenda's rejection and hesitation, he was ill prepared for her attempt at flirting. In an attempt to match him at his ability to engage others in conversation, she took a chance and asked him for crackers instead of the phone. She looked pale and awkward, a woman with a weak plan. Thinking she was sick, he teased her for being out drinking so late the night before.

I caught my breath, guessing what pain those stinging words brought. She had let her guard down and this was his response. His brother later stormed into the break room, accusing him of hurting her. "What a jerk you are," he said. "She was trying to flirt."

"Flirt?" he asked, stunned. His heart wept at the stupid mistake. If he could somehow remove that one bad day, he would convince her that his adoration would last until she was old and hogging the blankets. Maybe this was finally it, he hoped. Finally, the moment had come where the two of them could respect each other and enjoy a real date. She was at last comfortable with him, and he still adored her as he had the first day he saw her. He rushed back upstairs to invite her for a movie date.

"FRIDAY, APRIL 23, 1999" He had made sure to write it in big letters near the top of the page. That was the day he finally took possession of his dream, the day he could gaze into her eyes and whisper how much he had longed for this moment, pining for her affection. They chose the movie called *Cruel Intentions.* He nervously ached for this woman who intoxicated him. He went on to write how he missed her when he could not hold her hand and smell her hair. Her smile assured him he could fly over the moon. She was his rock. Despite his cheery optimism and her practical realism, they knew they would be loyal and encourage each other.

That simple first date grew into a stabbing pain that filled his stomach when she was out of town or on the road. She was independent and he was not possessive, but he needed her. He loved the way they complemented each other while they were among friends. She was his ally, his soul mate. Whatever they had to face as a couple, they would conquer.

They understood that a house took time to buy, and the picket fence may be a far-off dream. He was confident that they could build it together. She was becoming his every breath, and their hearts seemed to share a rhythm. He wanted to linger in the moonlight, clasping her hands and caressing her back. He wanted to know that she was there, forever, to hold him tight.

"It is funny," he wrote in his fascinating journal, "she was so small, but when she hugged me during 9/11, I knew everything would be all right."

That is why when they had aspirations of education, they endured the struggles every couple face in enhancing their career potential. They were young, and wanted careers rather than working in a casino, which did not offer a life for a couple who wanted a stable family. JR was accepted for university in the city and Brenda went to college in another town. It became difficult to be apart. However, Brenda was determined that it would work. She drove back to town every weekend to be at his side. They needed to earn their education and there would be sacrifices to attain that goal. The travel was worth the sacrifice in order to gain marriage, a family, and most of all a home. Not just a quaint house. They wanted something that was theirs, free of college roommates coming in and out, and a parking stall for as many vehicles as they chose to own. Being from the reserve, they wanted to live in a safe neighbourhood, to sit together enjoying a little bit of life in a home where one day their children could prance around the yard telling the cat not jump on them. They were becoming the couple who could envision what the Aboriginal community was losing.

JR planned a trip to Edmonton with Brenda and his parents, hoping to convince her it was merely a shopping trip. She was excited – going to a mall with his family – how could a woman not be happy? First, he thought, he must have a ring. Asking his mother for advice, JR and his mother snuck off to the local jewellery store to choose a ring. They savoured the moment of shared excitement - until they saw Brenda roaming the mall nearby. Afraid his roommate had told her where they were, he needed to think fast as she entered the jewelry store, happy to see them both.

"Uh, hey, Brenda," he fumbled. "My mother is going to buy a watch for me."

Brenda wondered at the odd purchase. Why would he put that financial burden on his mother? JR and his mother were also worried – more than she realized. Somehow, now JR needed the money for a ring and a $400 watch. His mother sweetly suggested each pay half. Relieved, Brenda and his mother went to the restaurant for a bite to eat. As they left the jewellery store, Brenda wondered why the clerk was smiling at her so goofily.

He could not wait until they reached Edmonton. His parents agreed to tape the proposal. He knew she would jump into his arms, declare him her immortal beloved, and promise him the world. As they drove, his friend called to tell him he had become engaged. As Brenda listened, he declared, "Are you sure, man? Marriage is forever." As he joked with his friend, Brenda's heart sunk. The man she believed in shunned marriage. Asking her later why she was so ill, she reminded him that marriage with the right person develops a deeper level of intimacy. He agreed – if a man had really found the right one, he said. He had destabilized her. She was left feeling monotone, and questioning . . . .

After a day of shopping, JR wanted to surprise Brenda. She loved cats, and it had broken her heart when the cat he gave her at the beginning of their relationship went missing. When she entered his parents' hotel room, he had a sweet fluffy kitten waiting for her. Enthralled by the little kitten, she immediately forgave his ignorant comment about marriage. Caught up with the adorable animal, she ignored JR. Surely they could not leave the helpless kitten in this inhumane cage. She began making preparations for the kitten to roam the bathroom. The mewling kitten had needed comfort while they indulged themselves at the restaurant.

JR began to see how easily distracted a caregiver can be, and quickly dropped to one knee in the hope of regaining her attention. When she eventually turned toward him, he asked the most vulnerable question a man could ask, reaching for her hand and her heart for eternity. He wanted her, and he needed her. Waiting for her response, he became uneasy. His knee began to ache, and his breath seemed to dissipate. It felt like an eternity before Brenda spoke. She stared at him with a blank gaze, and he began to question his reason for being. At last she whispered, *"Yes."* He could once again smile. He had wooed her and won her.

The wedding day would be perfect, he gloated. She had found the ideal dress, and looked radiant. Every detail was in place, the bridesmaids in order, and a family to love and adore. Being First Nation, they would have a tepee for the ceremony. The guest list was acceptably pared. As he hung tiny Christmas-like lights on the tepee to make the event more romantic, he looked around to see if Brenda needed him. He had noticed earlier that she was not herself; now, she was apparently missing.

Suddenly, pale, he began to question her absence. *Cold feet?* He began to panic, suddenly uncertain of their commitment, wondering about the walk down the aisle. Why else would she not help decorate for the day every bride dreams of? Thoughts raced through his mind as his insecurity accelerated. He asked his friends, nonchalantly, about her whereabouts, nervously glancing around the room. Sensing that perhaps a family emergency had distracted her, he agreed to go golfing with his father and brother when they offered to take his mind off the wedding preparations. It was raining on the golf course, yet relaxing. His father was able to relieve his insecurity and doubts a little.

JR told himself not to worry; she loved him and would be there. He stood at the altar dressed, spit polished and ready for eternity. When she did not appear, his heart sunk. He begged God to please bring her home to his arms. He waited . . . for what seemed like hours. A messenger walked up the aisle, carrying a white envelope. He hoped he would not faint. He could not endure the heartache of her leaving him on the most important day of their lives, when the two were destined to become intertwined. Slowly he opened the card, bracing himself for possible rejection. Instead, he read a beautiful love note from his soul mate. She would be there, it read, and no matter what they experienced in life, she would always walk down the aisle to embrace him. When she entered the room shortly afterward, he was breathless. She would be there, walking down the aisle, ready with arms to embrace him.

"She was beautiful," read his journal. "My wife is absolutely beautiful."

## Chapter Twelve

# CEO

## We Meet

"Just go see her!" Elaine hollered.

"I told Georgina that you were coming, don't be so chicken."

I was to walk up to the dialysis unit where a health director waited for four hours, three times a week, attached to a machine because her kidneys were not functioning. Knowing that nonchalance might not be well received, I would introduce myself as my mother's daughter. She had the opportunity of working with her up north, and my insecurities removed all shame about name-dropping. Since the political leaders within her sphere were often time conscious and demanding, I purposefully assured myself that I would respect her time. The health administrators I had experienced in the past looked unapproachable, overwhelmed by budgets and misguided drug expenditures.

I wanted to know how a woman succeeded in an aboriginal community where women have very defined roles. Hoping to learn from her experience, I had prepared numerous questions about how the northern health district functioned.

Many people are unaware of how the provincial and federal governments divide the responsibility of health care in the northern regions or on First Nations reserves. I was also intrigued by this woman with a reputation for getting the job done, considering the health district I worked for has owed production assistants *retro pay* for eighteen months. Union leaders and office administrators often ensured employees that the "process was progressing"; yet, we saw very little of that progress matching the speed of growth in Saskatoon.

Georgina and her husband had been well respected in every community they had lived in. Her husband functioned as vice president of the Dené people before he died, and a building was named in his honour.

Looking forward to interviewing Georgina about her role as a health director from the north, I was overly excited. My trips north normally required ten hours in snow, or rather, slush with rain. There was very little chance of meeting with professionals having *Northern* insight I could draw upon. Instead, I often spent most of my visiting time eating.

Professionals in the north were not keen on discussing theories, as they faced the need for practical problem-solving daily. They were mainly concerned about solutions and adapting tools created for those in power in the city. Survival became the primary focus when it was cold, and the surrounding small towns provided only necessities. Salaries were spent on expensive arctic coats, and 4x4 all-terrain vehicles that guzzled gas but kept them out of the ditches.

Surviving in the North and progressing as a professional were the keys to success. Titles mean very little to many of the locals, who work hard and spend their evenings at the *Trapper's Restaurant* wolfing down the best chili in the North. Warming themselves with hot coffee, they chat about politics.

What defines an eminent career woman in the North is her ability to lead while earning respect. Georgina MacDonald was known as a health director who spoke with wisdom and caused an impact. Her followers adored her; her listening ear was remembered by many. Georgina is an elder who left a legacy for young women to aspire to. She is one who overcomes, a widow with a story.

When I had arrived, Georgina seemed startled by my height, and unprepared for my appearance. She had known my mother for a couple of years when she was working and living in Fond du Lac. I did not resemble my mother and she had questioned who I was. Then she heard a resemblance in our laughter. I told her that my mother was still mad about the "fat club." Georgina howled with delight, and reminisced with me about how much fun her club had been for all the ladies.

## The Fat Club

Georgina, who had been fighting diabetes, led a group of Northern women into a healthier lifestyle through a group called the "fat club." My mother questioned Georgina's choice of name, suggesting that a name more sensitive to women struggling with their weight might be chosen. Georgina simply looked at her inquisitively, stroked her chin and responded with a subtle, to-the-point: "Are we in denial?" Apparently my mother was, because she joined the club—which proved to be full of many such truthful moments, as well as life improving information. My mother lost twenty pounds that spring, which is hard when most residents in the north hibernate like bears all winter. Georgina was neither pushy nor aggressive, she just wanted to inspire women to value their health. She offered practical solutions, trying leading others by example.

Georgina had no personal agenda but simply desired to empower women as she empowered herself. She had enjoyed life in a residential school and returned to the north. Hearing her reminisce, I found her joy contagious. She had an easy-going personality, yet it was evident that she was a visionary leader.

Until her illness made her too tired, she had travelled monthly to Regina for meetings, while juggling the responsibilities of northern health care. I did not know what CEO meant, but I could see by the impact she had on me that she was very influential. Within half an hour, I was filling my day planner with phone numbers of people I was to contact.

As she spoke her hands moved, beating time to the shrill beeping of the dialysis machine. In spite of ugly tubes attached to her shoulder, she was still mesmerizing. With her dark piercing eyes she looked directly into me and flashed an enchanting smile. I did not know that we were equal in height until she stood up. Later when my interviews had progressed towards a friendship, she was constricted to a chair. I had seen my grandmother attached to machines for years before she died, and felt a natural sympathy for Georgina, despite her obvious strength.

Diabetes and kidney failure often robs even the strongest of people of the air they breathe. If their spirit remains unbroken by the illness, the machines become annoying and the diet restricting. The loss of their home as they travel to one of the few dialysis units is heartbreaking. Then there is all that time lost, sitting, thinking and listening to the conversations of nurses who become all too familiar. But somehow Georgina was not bitter, attached to the beeping box, she remained hopeful and entertaining.

"About to go to see the optometrist," she announced. She had been to bingo, while straining to see the balls, discovered her eye sight was weakening. "I am getting Mutant Ninja Turtle glasses," she said with a broad smile. Confused, because I had not seen the television show since childhood, visions of her walking the ward like a turtle frightened me. Being my mother's age, she had probably watched many episodes with her own children as they were growing up. Noticing my concern, she explained that she looked like a Ninja Turtle when wearing dark rimmed glasses.

"Oh," I giggled. "For a minute I thought that you had been working in the health industry for too long, that travelling sucked the life out of northern employees, and you were slowing down."

She had been North most of her life. She loved the people and she loved the North. I could empathize. My own encounters left me longing for "the bush," with Arctic winds reddening my cheeks. There are no functioning renal units in the north, which means Georgina had to go on disability and leave her community for Saskatoon. Leaving home for the city can be mind numbing for young people, but for an older woman established in her career, it is crushing.

When her homesickness becomes overwhelming, Georgina travels to a park north of Prince Albert to walk through the bush. Touching my arm gently, she assured me: the drive would be easy if I missed the winter winds. *Is it possible to miss those winds*? Yes, I feel a calm deep in my soul when I am quiet enough to hear the wind through the tall trees.

"Was it a hard transition?" I asked, knowing how difficult moving to the city can be.

"I am near my daughter and I love that," she smiled. She talked highly of her Gennifer, the quiet force behind her success. Chuckling, she told me how her daughter wore Shrek ears at Halloween to make her mother laugh. Forgetting she was wearing them, she answered the door. The politician canvassing for votes found it extremely difficult to focus while she nodded in her huge green "dress up" ears. Gennifer shared her mother's sense of humour. They delighted in the simplicity of life, enjoying whatever time was granted to them. As an administrator in the North, I could tell by the way her mother described Gennifer that she, too, would probably become a nation changer.

## The Chicks

As a child who attended residential school and enjoyed her time away from home, Georgina explained that her home life was neither safe nor enriching, although she loved her mother. She recalled having to sleep in a frigid home in the sub-arctic winters, before being taken to residential schools. Sleeping with a butcher knife jammed in the door to ward off intruders, it was difficult to feel safe while her mother entertained people she did not know. At least at her new home, she enjoyed three meals a day instead of one, and did not live in fear as she slept. She described her Christian-based residential school as a refuge. She still kept in touch with her family, and still had fond memories of her school.

In those new surroundings she was treated like a little girl, full of life and adventure. She was treated as though the school was her home to roam free, as long as she picked peas every day during the summer. Georgina and her friends could race off to the river to spend summer vacations dreaming. Always a dreamer even as a young girl, she had followers hoping to share an adventure with her.

She seemed to be the type who did not find trouble, it followed her. While accompanying an adult to town, she bought a magazine at the post office and smuggled it into her room. As a preteen, it was very important to look as beautiful as the models in the magazine. Her little "chicks," as she called them, followed her around the school, and wanted to look through the magazine too. Her *little chicks* were three scared, little girls who had not been away from home before, and she taught them how to function in the residence. She taught them how to make their beds, clean their rooms and put milk on the tables before supper, if that was their assigned task.

Reading her secret magazine was Georgina's only connection to the beauty industry outside that small prairie town. In this small community, fashion and eastern city values were unappreciated. After reading the *banned* magazine with her friends, the girls were convinced that if she shaved off their eye brows, they would grow back even fuller and lusher. The models' photos united *the chicks* in their resolve to look like the beautiful women with dainty thin eyebrows. One day, when they sauntered into the food hall, their care providers stared in horror. Luckily, they chalked up the facial baldness to one of "Georgina's ideas." Apparently, her chicks stayed loyal, although it took some time to look like *chicks* again.

It was intriguing how she went from being a girl raised in a rural residential school to eventually directing a health district. It seemed so contrary to the humorous tales she told. When I first moved to Saskatchewan, most people I encountered were angry about their residential school experience. These were people who walked down the street asking for quarters; people who threatened to beat up others for looking at them "funny." I had never met anyone who was not limited by their past, or perhaps I had never been in the sphere of accomplished people.

## Changes

I could not help but admire this woman who went back to university, with the support of her husband to get a teaching degree; then went on to earn a Director of Health position, which is usually held by men.

After her husband died, she said softly, she did not want to teach anymore. Georgina loved teaching, but I could see how she loved her husband deeply. After his funeral and her time to mourn, she simply needed a change. She needed a new challenge, and a place to call home.

"I am sure that you were a great teacher," I said purposefully. "You are very animated and interesting to watch."

"Teaching was a joy," she said seriously, "up until the late eighties,"

"What happened after the Bands took over?" I probed curiously.

"We lost a golden opportunity," she sighed with regret.

She went on to explain. While teaching, she picked out her own books; she would read them, during story time, to the young students learning English as a second language. She also taught science, social studies and history. They had the freedom to teach whatever curriculum they wanted when the Band was in charge, a wonderful idea if the teachers are responsible and progressive. Educators had the opportunity to speak with the community, encouraging parents to be involved in their children's education. If they wanted changes in the educational system, they could voice their opinions.

Instead, there became a focus on Math and English, to appease the post-secondary requirements of the province. Subject repetition brought disdain from the students, who were already finding school irrelevant and unrewarding. First Nations children have always learned through storytelling. Principles have always been woven into stories, offering young students visual and auditory lessons that enhance their culture.

I remarked how I had I noticed that teachers, like young nurses, came to do "their two years" to make money, get certified, and gain experience in order to land a "well coveted position" in the city. They were not always interested in reaching the children or trying to inspire them.

The ones who had disdain for the North and were indifferent to that lifestyle, kept to themselves, focusing on core subjects even if the children skipped classes out of boredom. But not all of the new teachers were indifferent. It was when I spent my summer there, it became evident who would stay and who would vanish once a better opportunity arose.

Some new residents simply found it difficult to live on an isolated reserve with only a winter road made of mud leading to the nearest town. Some were ill prepared for what a "fly-in" reserve was, not ready to fly in a four-seater plane with a two suitcase limit. Professionals, accustomed to the conveniences the city offered, did not realize that they could not just return home for the weekend on a whim. Groceries they were accustomed to in the city were too expensive to fly into the reserve. The store sold only what the cost of shipping allowed. There were apples, oranges, and heads of lettuce and carrots for produce.

Georgina explained in her authoritative teaching voice, how educators could bring math and English skills into their science, social studies classes and projects if they were willing to stimulate the kids. It was possible, with a little creativity, to coerce them into reading if the books were colourful and offered projects that integrated their learning. She had worked on a board in Prince Albert that helped fund projects beneficial to both the reserve and the school. Project leaders only needed to submit a proposal; for the sake of their children's learning. Teachers should incorporate oral, visual, and kinesthetic types of learning—but visual methods are best for this culture.

I remembered how my mother taught cooking classes to the young women on the reserve each Friday night. The young women thrived with these hands-on, visual lessons that they could easily remember. Single teenage moms became excited even when learning something as basic as spaghetti and meatballs. Georgina and her husband enjoyed being able to work with the teacher and their hands, just as they had in the past with the elders. Aboriginal people learned best through example and by following a teacher.

The children would memorize songs that had hand actions, and remember vividly the facial expressions of their teachers. Once a lesson had a little creativity, they were all very eager to learn. That is why Georgina chose colourful books that would catch their attention, and read them to the children like a seasoned storyteller. She knew to feed their curiosity with details. She chose her words wisely to prevent children from shaving off their eyebrows as she had. Encouragement on the reserves was scarce, and often the children took to heart whatever was spoken to them. They remembered the tone in which something was said, and the few teachers who believed in them. They cherished the attention and enjoyed praise.

After hearing how deeply she enjoyed teaching, I found it ironic that Georgina became an administrator for the health district, then a health director. She spoke lovingly of her husband—getting acquainted after tripping over him and then courting. They had a happy marriage, she assured me, and he was her rock, the anchor that got her through teacher's college and onward to become the first woman on her reserve to earn a degree. His strength and admiration helped her succeed at her goals. Even the Dené Aboriginals wanted him to be chief, yet he refused; he said "Chiefs lose their jobs too quickly." Instead, he became Vice President of the Dené, where he could help to facilitate, offering stability.

Both leaders, John and Georgina were active in their community. They enlisted volunteers easily because they had a reputation for organizing memorable youth events, and were known for genuinely caring about people. When I asked again why she left teaching, she simply looked down with a softness I had not seen before and responded thoughtfully:

"I just didn't want to do what I was doing when I lost him. I just needed to do something completely different."

She expected me to understand; but I could not understand the loss of a good man this widow had suffered. To lose half of me would have broken my resolve. Her soul mate was lost, yet she was not. She would continue the journey until hers ended. Going into something new felt awkward she admitted, but challenge revived her heart. She was determined that she would always bloom wherever she was planted, not waste away like an uprooted flower in the summer sun.

"*It's funny,*" she said quietly, "when my husband and I packed for our move to Fond du Lac, we noticed a horse just wandering around our abandoned village, feeding on the empty lawns."

"Was it brown?" I gasped. "Did the horse scare you?"

"I am sure it was brown." she replied, puzzled by my paleness. "Scared? It was time for change, we were moving to our new home where we could work together. The horse stayed in the abandoned mining town."

Sensing that our conversation had become awkward, she put my mind at ease by changing the subject. We lingered over our conversation, passing the afternoon with humour. I enjoyed her company, and hearing how she had finally become the health director in the

North. Funding was limited, efficiency was needed, and travelling was difficult for the northern health director. Georgina boarded a six-seater plane once a month, landed in Stoney, boarded another small plane, landed in Prince Albert, then waited for the next flight to Saskatoon (which was scheduled for the convenience of the southern travellers.)

Deplaning in Saskatoon, again she waited. Then she boarded another plane to Regina to spend a day of travel to attend meetings. It was difficult: four days worth of travelling for one afternoon meeting when a provincial minister attended. She travelled the distance to ensure that people in the North were remembered. By speaking at the meeting she reminded everyone that the Northern community existed. When asked how they could accommodate her more, she suggested meetings in Stoney. *Perhaps a meeting in Prince Albert was half way?* They just chuckled, used to her humour.

I commiserated when she told me about travelling expenses. Having travelled myself often, I knew how much gas and lodging cost, and how much time was spent on the roads and in those little airplanes. Tossed by winter winds, flights were not always pleasure cruises. It was daunting to watch a pilot de-ice the wings by hitting them with a broom stick and assuring us we would make it to Edmonton. On those flights, I not only repented for anything I had done wrong, I repented on behalf of my sister's wrongs too, in case God was watching.

The memory of the long drives and bumpy flights now showed on Georgina's face as she sat alone in her hospital chair. The machine beeps and I am secretly relieved that she is still alive. When I am by her side, she is a rock full of optimism. Yet when she thinks I am gone, she sleeps. She sleeps because she gave us her youth. She sleeps, because after years of building a community, she now commutes three hours, three times a week to the only renal unit in northern Saskatchewan.

"If I win the lottery," she said with a chuckle "I will build a renal unit near my community."

I believe that she would. She has the tenacity and the vision needed to help a community weakened by an unwanted and often overlooked disease. Keeping still during my last visit, she mentioned that my generation has lost the finesse of negotiation. She commented how young adults prefer bold confrontation to peaceful problem solving. I could not fathom how finesse might benefit a middle-aged woman fighting for her life, yet it seemed to be the skill she needed to survive all of life's changes.

As I sat in the uncomfortable visitor's chair, I did not see a patient who orders cheese and crackers from the cafeteria three times a week. I saw a CEO who has paid her dues, loving her husband and children with all that she was. I saw a First Nations elder who had built a community she believed in with determination. I saw a CEO who had left a legacy to inspire women.

She smiled with her eyes that day; she smiled with her eyes everyday. Looking up with that delightful grin, she suggested that I return to visit her again. *Of course I was going to visit my new friend, to protect her however I could.* She and I would escape the city and walk in the bush, forgetting the past as we laughed. We would stroll carefree in the summer, because that chair is not her home.

## Chapter Thirteen

# Beauty from Ashes

# Lost

The golden plains where warriors once valiantly fought still offer an exhilarating journey for the adventurous. Feeling as though my journey in Saskatoon was ending, I submitted written notice to my landlord. The cost of living increases that accompanied the city's new prosperity had crippled my dream. Posting ads for my cherished furniture on the Internet only added to the cloud of despair. With each bartering reply, my rejection deepened. Carefully wrapping my European teacups, I felt the northern winds of change beckon.

Wanting to retreat home to northern Alberta, I gazed out my window longingly. Birds fluttered, and I could see spring warmth finally surfacing. I would simply move forward, allowing the glow of the prairies to lighten my memories.

There were few positions available in the North; even the oil boom was declining. My heart wept each time I ended a visit at the northern community that had knitted my soul with theirs. One could not live amongst the fearless survivors of the North without being changed. Even as I packed, I perused recipes, anticipating the next potluck.

Northern towns where pioneers worked so hard to earn respect have little patience for falsehood. Encountering the viscous mud of the prairies, pioneers fought for survival as they travelled northward. When winter winds howled, the only beauty left was their inner strength. The tranquil prairie evenings purged the young of their independence, rewarding the aged for their wisdom.

Daring to visit my family each spring, I challenged the clenching soil of the north. The four-seater plane ride left me weakened; I yawned to prevent permanent eardrum damage from the roar of the engines. The land of the living skies had revived my dreams while soaring through the mist, embracing risk. The North was brutish, yet mystical. Greeted by dented taxis, I endured countless journeys, driven towards desolate communities built out of the bush. Dirt roads wound on and on like a maze, exposing lakes covered by a haze of black flies and mosquitoes. Dry air saturated the lungs with a fine dust. The rickety bridges jangled my nerves. Mud crept up my ankles, permanently staining my clothing, while the sun baked it dry. The reek of rotting wood and green slime signalled yet another swamp.

The journey required multiple skills; individuals had to adapt to each emergency or unexpected circumstance. Between the buildings, the clay soil was knee high in spring, and sticky like honey. If I did not step carefully, my boots would stick, as though the tarry brown substance remembered me. The nurses, little fluffy wet ducks waddling back and forth in formation, followed whoever discovered the best path to the nursing station.

On the reservation, the dust settled, and the heat lingered like an untold secret. Local dogs growled at the distant wild packs, their howls unsettling at dusk.

Grime permeated every part of my body on each

northern trip, like the stench of rotting garbage. To be on the reservation was a test of survival, not only because it was physically challenging, but because it reminded each adventurer they were interdependent in an otherwise independent world.

A gentle and introspective people, the Cree were once fierce warriors. Today their curious children giggle, fascinated by each new face, and reach to touch a cheek, a lip or the strange coloured hair.

The creative young women, if asked kindly, would offer their opinion. Rarely would they intrude on a conversation or argue with a stranger. Catching an Aboriginal woman's smile was a beautiful rarity – like dew on the petals of a wild rose.

## Dreamers

That is why I found Rosie so intriguing. Her unassuming personality was unforgettable. She was a hard worker. Her culture did not allow her to look deeply in the eyes of another, yet her presence was powerful. She was gentle, but organized the clinic like an unstoppable force. She appreciated the uncomplicated life, demanding little. Tucked away in her heart lay a simple faith in God, attending Mass each week. She was plain to look at, her eyes weathered by unforgiving winds. Her teeth had grown beige, evidence of isolation in the little northern community.

Like the forest, she was full of familiar tones and the smell of wildflowers that refresh early morning hikers. She loved deeply, and sacrificed for her 10 children, one of whom was disabled. Embracing the life of permanent parenthood, she celebrated each victory her children achieved. Her diligence would be rewarded with a well-earned retirement. Her community of people greatly respected her patience with her child.

Everyone who came to work in the little community soon realized that William was Rosie's soul mate. They knew, as he gently brushed by her in the hallway or smiled sheepishly around a corner, he was a complicated man. Helping visiting professionals feel welcome and settled, William's eyes could ease the stress of being so isolated. His sense of humour was dry, and he saw the beauty in life's little endeavours. Gentle with Rosie, he spoke lovingly of her children.

William was a comely man, made handsome by his servant's heart. He believed in earning an honest wage, proudly showing Rosie each pay stub. He was stable – in a community where change was constant. Few could endure; they would escape as soon as their contracts were complete.

The couple had spent years building a beautiful log cabin that many dream of. Building a log cabin takes a great deal of dedication and hard work. Theirs was a three-year project, requiring immense planning and diligence. First, they would walk far into the bush to size trees. If their trapline had been 100 miles away, the job would have been even more arduous. They needed three different sizes: trees smaller than the round of a hand, others the size of two wrists together, and lastly, the largest – the root of much back pain and muscle ache. The skill was in looking at the tree to see if it was straight, round, and tall enough. Next, when the time was right for the trees to be cut without causing splits in the wood, they chopped the trees, often unequally, but with luck, free of knots for the labourers.

In preparation, they skinned the trees by hand. This time-consuming stripping process often resulted in nicked and bleeding skin. When the bark was taken off at the wrong time, Rosie felt that oozing sap penetrate each skin pore and crevice. Wincing with compassion, William touched her burning hand. She held his hand firmly, reminding him her love was forever. This was their dream; it made materialism irrelevant. The skinning incident gave Rosie an excuse to run her fingers through his hair.

In summer, she would pour cold tea into glasses as they lingered near the porch. Smiling, he would watch her hips sway as she danced for him alone. They were enamored by each other, and by the dream of their home.

Wisdom gained during the building process is shared among First Nations people. A cabin on the reserve is a risky dream earned by sacrifice. There is no house insurance – not even for a project that takes years. In the past, two logs were tied onto an inverted riding saddle, dragged by horses through the trees and marsh, and back to the village. In the absence of horses, winches were used. Chains and stamina were needed for the arduous task. As technology advanced, skidoos and quad runners replaced the horses, slowly dragging the uneven logs home, coupled with u-hooks to prevent snags. Folly burns out motors, and gasoline is not cheap.

William and Rosie chopped, skinned, marched, hauled, and sweated to build their retirement home. They would not allow exhaustion to consume them like an angry wolf, until their cabin stood tall in the middle of the community: complete, solid, and marvellous. The cabin was not just a building with skinned logs and precisely placed walls. The cabin was their retirement home, where they would watch their family run in the yard.

William and Rosie had sacrificed for their retirement. They had put away their wages, purchasing items only as necessary. Taking very few trips into town, they fought the madness of isolation. Each winter, huddling closely together, they caught glimpses of each other's distress. Holding each other, they rested together. Clutching the dream of summertime, William told jokes as he sipped his tea. The exhaustion of raising a challenged child would ease slightly once their new rooms were secure. William and Rosie focused on their prime objective, while others travelled. They hoped for the best, while others surrendered to good enough. Their faithfulness became a testimony for all visitors.

Once they had brought the logs to their building site, cupping them was difficult. If the moon-shaped logs were not properly placed, angry rains and pelting snow would penetrate the building. Fifty-dollar garage sale windows had to be firmly placed in the space carved for them; otherwise, humidity and mildew would ravage their retirement dream. Each step offered opportunities for bickering, but only strengthened their resolve. They were past the age of selfish expectations. They had lived through years of disappointment, accepting and supporting each other. As they bound together logs, William would turn his head, catching her eye, aching when amorous whispers ceased.

Together they created a refuge, a place to dwell in comfort as they aged. Each handcrafted detail inspired others nearing the end of their careers. Retirement would be a time of joy, not of struggle. It would be a time of reflection and relaxation, not of demands and obligations. Their home would reveal their timeless passion. They had furnished it with a new bed frame and mattress, and delicate lamps discovered with childlike excitement. Photos capturing beautiful memories were meaningfully placed where William could regain calm after an evening of work.

They were on a reservation in the remote bush, yet managed to build a unique home, a home that reflected who they were. He didn't mind her clutter; she didn't mind his tools. They were united, dedicated, their bond proven. Those who met William were happy for him. We were inspired by their loyalty to each other, despite the scars and bumps on his forearms. Wanting to hear news of the cabin, I asked people of the community if their dream was now complete.

## Broken dreams

One afternoon, fiery flames roared like a black bear throughout the community. Rosie's heart sank. She instinctively knew that it was her home on fire. Crying as she ran out the door, her co-workers crowded out behind her, gasping with horror. She was desperate to rescue what she could of her dream.

Everyone paused, quietly counting the cost of the tragedy striking the community. The air was cool, the whispers faint. Office workers looked out windows, catching a glimpse of the misfortune.

All work came to a halt as everyone watched the dreaded fire truck race to the rising flames and black smoke. Thinking his daughter was trapped in the cabin, William frantically yanked at the front door. Overcome by the smoke and heat, he fell back from the inferno, while friends leaped forward to pull him away. The fire truck came, but only to control the spread of the flames and prevent further damage to the community. Getting the needed water to this fire site was not even a consideration. There dream was all over in 10 minutes.

Black ashes lay in piles, thin wisps of smoke still rising.

Fires strike a community with the impact of a tornado, but with more severe financial repercussions. No insurance company offers fire insurance plans to these isolated communities.

To me, the cabin had represented community strength, within a region of cruel emergencies. Even though I was only a casual visitor, I felt protective of the cabin because of what it represented. We all believed that if William and Rosie could build a cabin from trees in the woods, there was hope for our own dreams of building a home. Despite their financial limitations, owning a home was inspiring. They were *trabalahars* in the middle of the Canadian forest.

By the noon hour, only sympathy, sorrow and grief over such an injustice lingered. Some diverted their eyes, stunned by Rosie and William's loss. Occasionally a youth winced, perhaps thinking that the soul mates had wasted years trying. Others felt ashamed, knowing they were not in a position to help. The cabin had been engulfed by the fiery claws of hell while family members closed frightened eyes. The community watched their hope burn to ashes. *Perhaps, once lost is always lost.*

The couple stood in helpless shock, while they watched all they had saved for, all they had worked for, reduced to smouldering black rubble.

For minutes afterward, William sat there like an abandoned chief, feeling betrayed by the earth, seeing his time and effort wasted and consumed.

The community instinctively knew that it would take everything within Rosie to dream again; it would take everything within William to hope again. It was a strength and endurance incomprehensible to the youngsters who gawked shamelessly. The children watched with mere curiosity, unable to fathom why this dream was so important. Only true survivors like Allie could grasp the impact of the ashes swirling about their legs. She had developed the strength required to climb from a wheelchair onto her bed, not taking for granted the effort to maintain hope. She celebrated each simple victory.

Like warriors in the middle of smoldering ashes, the couple stood united and began to rebuild. First, they would restore their lives, then they would rebuild their home.

## Restoration

Only days later, William and Rosie drove through the rough terrain as if embarking on a valiant mission. Protecting her back with his hand, they entered the bush to size trees. The trees must again be gathered along and within their own trap line area. Again they persevered through the - long process of tromping through the bush.

William valued Rosie's opinion as she pointed to potentials. Years ago, they had forgiven each other for their differences, bringing peace to a weathered relationship. Each had surpassed blaming, embracing unity instead.

William held his soul mate, gently wiping tears from her eyes. Rebuilding their retirement home would require still more sacrifice. It would involve teamwork, ensuring they built a home – not just a house. They spent hours in detestable mud and marsh, enduring spring humidity and the torment of thousands of mosquitoes.

Without complaint or sarcasm, they worked together once again, skinning more than 30 hundred-foot logs. Each one left a painful scratch on Rosie's forearms, cruelly reminding her of the black ashes now sitting on her land. Despite the taunting memories, they remained diligent, slaving for hours and days. They carved off the bark without solace from nature and without financial help usually offered to those who suffer misfortune. They would not surrender, would not die of heartache. The couple confronted life with a fortitude few could muster.

Co-workers gasped in shock when Rosie arrived with dark, pink lines covering her forearms. Afraid she had been burned in the fire, they gathered around her concerned for her well-being. Grinning with defiance, she turned over her arms, revealing caked blood near her wrists. Those battle wounds, she announced, were the result of skinning.

News of the fire brought tears to my eyes. Unlike Rosie, I had allowed the past to rob my hope. Being lost was the result of my own rejection. Striving to rescue relationships from the fire had left me devastated, ending my journey in the prairies. Yet Rosie knew that her journey was far from finished.

The aging couple clung to their faith in Christ and to each other. Once again, they became a testimony of hope. They were not lost angels like my generation, wandering the prairies in search of a dream. Rosie and William rebuilt their dream within their own community.

For a brief moment, we are offered an *Encounter* to learn who we really are. It is a special moment when eyes are widened by the courage one needs to sustain hope. This aging couple, consumed by understandable grief, kept building. Soul mates, blaming no one, sacrificed time for their dream. United, they discovered their strength by protecting each other.

It was a glorious morning for the community when William and Rosie began to rebuild. It was evidence that God could – and would – restore beauty from ashes.